"Michael A. Caparrelli, PhD (abd) is a prolific and prophetic writer who possesses the unique gift of communication and the ability to bring clarity to complexity. I can count on one hand preachers that possess Michael's literary and oratory skills, integrity and transparency. We, who know the man personally, recognize what an intellectual and prophetic maverick he truly is—a special gift is among us for sure."

—Bishop Jeffery A. Williams, D.Min, MPA

"Don't hesitate for one moment to welcome Michael A. Caparrelli, PhD (abd) to speak. You won't be disappointed. He is a man regenerated by the Spirit of God and wanting to convey the same to others is his passion. As a man of great character and quality, he is highly interested in people and his audiences walk away better than they arrived. Michael speaks with both humor and intellect having been highly gifted by God to serve the body of Christ in every kind of venue."

—Pasco A. Manzo President/CEO Teen Challenge
New England & New Jersey

Pen Your Pain Into Parables

A TOOL FOR RECOVERY

Michael A. Caparrelli, *PhD. abd*

Published by UNMUTED Publications

Visit: unmuted.app
Contact: unmuted777@gmail.com

Back Cover Photo: Rebecca Daniele
(Facebook: *Radiance by Rebecca Photography*)
Interior illustration: Simone Spruce at *simonespruce.com*
Book Design: wordsintheworks.com

A specially-formatted workbook is available
online to accompany this book:
Pen Your Pain Into Parables–A Tool for Recovery Workbook

Please join our *Pain Into Parables Facebook Book club* at
Facebook.com/mcaparrelli

Dedication

For my children, Ashley, Michael, Hannah and Olivia.
May the Lord use the heartaches
of this life to make you *better* rather than *bitter*.

Foreword

Narrative thinking is a lost art in the church. Jesus spoke to us in parables (narratives). He along with all of the authors of the books of the Bible expressed themselves with narrative thinking under the Divine anointing of the Holy Spirit. The ability to tell one's story can be life-changing at times. The late poet Maya Angelou once stated, "There is no greater agony than bearing an untold story inside you." In his book *Pen Your Pain Into Parables*, Michael A. Caparrelli shares his personal journey, giving insights into his pain, his joy, and his learning along the road of life. Michael shares the narrative framework tool P.I.C.T.U.R.E. and tells how each one of us can use this tool in addressing painful memories and emotions in general.

In the second letter to the Corinthian church, the Apostle Paul writes the following (2 Corinthians 1:3-5 ESV): *Blessed be the God and Father of our Lord Jesus Christ, the Father of mercies and God of all comfort, who comforts us in all our affliction, so that we may be able to comfort those who are in any affliction, with the comfort with which we ourselves are comforted by God. For as we share abundantly in Christ's sufferings, so through Christ we share abundantly in comfort too.*

In these verses, Paul shares that as we are comforted through our pains or afflictions, we are to share that same comfort with others who are suffering as well, recognizing the comfort comes from the Creator Himself.

There is power in sharing your story with others. This book gives insights into how to frame your story for both personal and external impact and influence. As you let the Lord heal and comfort you through narrative tools, you will be better equipped to help others struggling as well. Galatians 6:2 says *Bear one another's burdens, and so fulfill the law of Christ.* In order to effectively help others in pain, you must receive the healing, strength and comfort from our Lord for your own pain. This book is filled with stories and tools to help you do that. My prayer for every reader is that our Savior Jesus Christ will envelop your life, transform your hearts and minds, and will show you the power of your life story and what God can do in a changed life.

—Gary Blackard President & CEO, Adult & Teen Challenge USA

INTRODUCTION
Framing Your Past

On display at Ford's Theater Museum in Washington, D.C., an oil painting a tad over three feet high and five feet wide, drapes from its interior walls, snatching the eye of every passerby. The picture vividly captures one of the most tragic moments in United States history; an occasion that converted a middle-age woman into a widow, three children into orphans and an entire nation into mourning. The work of art features the heart-wrenching sights that followed the assassination of President Abraham Lincoln, a scene in which his mortally-wounded body is transported through frantic flocks. The title of the masterpiece is *Lincoln Borne By Loving Hands* painted by an eye-witness, the German-immigrant Carl Bersch.

Who could have ever imagined this tragedy becoming such a work of art? Who could have ever envisioned this catastrophe becoming such a valuable artifact? Certainly, nobody on the streets of Washington, D.C. could have surmised that a moment so painful would become a masterpiece so profitable.

One of the primary reasons why the picture possesses such value is because it is framed in a customized exhibition-case, fully enclosed and climate-controlled. Without that encasement, the picture would depreciate its quality over the course of time, eventually losing its value and purpose. Also, without that encasement, the picture might not be as eye-catching to onlookers. *Lincoln Borne By Loving Hands* teaches us that...

*When you frame something the right way,
the most tragic moments become valuable artifacts.*

Chances are, you've had your share of catastrophic moments. Abandoned by a parent at birth, raised by an embittered single mother, abused by an alcoholic father, date-raped at a party, cheated on by your spouse, and the list goes on. All of these scenarios, during their occurrence, felt like the *end of the road;* little did you know that it was just a *bend in the road.* All of these circumstances felt like unsalvageable disasters that serve no purpose other than escalating your blood pressure and landing you on psych meds. All of these circumstances left you feeling like life would never be the same again. May I submit to you, that just like *Lincoln Borne By Loving Hands…*

*When you frame your painful past the right way,
the most tragic moments become valuable artifacts.*

A few years back, researchers from the University of Liverpool published a study that underscored the role of memories in generating certain emotions. The results showed that participants elevated their own moods by savoring positive memories, which in return caused them to feel less threatened by problems of the present and future. Perhaps you find it unlikely to savor such positive recollections given the nature of your horrific history. Maybe you deem it impossible to remember anything positive in light of all yesteryear's dysfunction. Here lies the purpose of this book—to help you interpret your past in such a way that it is no longer a tragedy that makes you *bitter*, but a testimony that makes you *better.*

Consider for a moment the possibility that if you frame your past the right way, your most tragic moments become valuable resources.

Painful or Profitable?

William Somerset Maugham, the English playwright and short story writer, once penned the account of an illiterate custodian who swept the floors of St. Peter's Church in London. Soon enough, one of the clerics fired the custodian after discovering he couldn't read. The downtrodden man brushed the dust off his feet and invested his skimpy savings into opening up a bicycle shop. Within a few years, the shop prospered, enabling him to open up a second shop. He continued buying bicycle shops until he accumulated hundreds of thousands of pounds. One day, the man's banker said to him after reviewing his assets, "You've done very well for an illiterate, but where would you be if you could read or write?" The illiterate man, looking back at that painful moment when he was ousted from the cathedral, said, "Well, I'd be janitor of St. Peter's church in Neville Square".

Let's face the facts. Many of us resentfully look back on moments when we were treated unjustly. If we were in the custodian's shoes, we might wallow in pity while looking back at being fired. For this custodian, he didn't look back and feel *rejection;* instead, he looked back and saw *re-direction.* When you look back at your painful moments, what do you see?

Your past is either utterly painful or exceedingly profitable, all depending upon how you frame it.

Before becoming president of South Africa, Nelson Mandela spent twenty-seven years unjustly locked up in prison because of his crusade for democracy. Some would argue he wasted twenty-seven years in prison. If you asked Mandela himself, he would tell you that those years weren't wasted time but invested time. In nearly three decades of incarceration, Mandela befriended prison guards from the other side of the ideological aisle. In his relationships with these guards, he listened to their viewpoints and developed an unusual compassion. According to Mandela himself, if it had not been for the twenty-seven years of being locked up, he would not have become the elevated leader of South Africa. The prison served as an incubator for empathy, understanding and compassion. Mandela's past was not just utterly painful but exceedingly beneficial…all because he framed it right.

How We Overcome.

In first century Palestine, Christians were persecuted on many levels by both the religious and secularists of that time period. Social ostracization, verbal onslaught, unjust imprisonment and even execution were the common perils of those who identified with Jesus Christ. Under such impending doom, the Apostle John writes the church a letter out of his own captivity known as the book of Revelation. In Revelation 12:11, John encourages the church to take hold of two firearms to overcome their fear and discouragement—the blood of the Lamb and the word of their testimony. This last phrase, "the word of their testimony" is another way of saying, "the vocal utterance of their story." Imagine, your story is not just comprised of words but weapons. *"They triumphed over him (Satan) by the Blood of the Lamb and the word of their testimony" (Rev. 12:11).*

In addition to what Jesus accomplished on the Cross, John encourages the church to triumph over evil by remembering and reciting their own story. If you ever forget your story, you leave behind a powerful weapon that keeps you safe when traversing through a dangerous terrain.

> *By remembering and reciting your story, you crush all fear, conquer all doubt and triumph over all evil.*

As it stands now, you may not be edified by your own story but provoked to shame, regret and trauma. This book is a tool that frames the painful moments of your past into great resources. All of the annoyances and grievances, the losses and the divorces, the abuse and misuse, the rejection and depression, make up your story. Each moment, even the worse moments, contributed a color to the masterpiece of your life.

By the end of this book, you will no longer despise the people, places and things of yesteryear. Nor will you feel ashamed of where you came from. In fact, it is impossible to love yourself and hate the experiences that shaped you. During this journey your past will become a well-spring of wisdom and strength that serves you all of the days of your life.

SOCIAL MEDIA EXERCISE: Please join our *Pain Into Parables Facebook Book club* at Facebook.com/mcaparrelli

CHAPTER ONE
Your Pain—The Aftereffects of Trauma

"Get over it!" That's what some folks glibly tell you after you suffered through years of abuse at the hands of a supposed caretaker. *"Move on with your life!"* That's what some people apathetically say after you survived domestic terrorism. *"Forget the past!"* That's what some friends callously tell you after enduring an upbringing in foster care, a childhood caught in the crossfire of two raging parents, a perverted touch from a pedophile uncle, a nightmare marriage to a cruel narcissist, etc. After all that agony, they tell you to go outside, cut down a tree, use the wood to build a bridge and *get over it.* Don't you wish it were that simple? Let's face it—what happens in a moment of time changes you for a lifetime. There are some instances from your past that you just can't get over.

To the well-meaning ignoramuses who make such statements, it would serve them well to conduct research on how trauma alters your brain chemistry. Neuroscientist Paul D. MacLean sheds light on trauma's effects upon the reptilian, the region of the brain that houses your survival instincts. During traumatic episodes, the reptilian assumes control of the brain causing your body to shift into survival mode; a mode in which you fight, flight or freeze in response to perceived threat. In some cases of trauma, the brain becomes stuck in this reptilian mode for long periods of time, hardly ever returning to the higher functions of emotional and critical intelligence. When this happens, it is impossible to get over what happened because it feels like it is still happening.

Trauma's aftereffect is like the ringing in your ear even after the shotgun blast fades...except the reverberation of trauma resumes even years later.

Maybe you made your best effort to run from the past. Perhaps you relocated to another city with less geographical reminders of your horrifying heritage. Quite possibly, you married into a new family in order to detach from your abusers. Or, maybe you lost yourself in a career or a substance in order to distance yourself from your history. Yet, you can't seem to escape the memories of days gone by. How do you *get over it* when you cannot seem to *get away from it?*

Like the victim in a scary movie running from the monster, you become startled when what's BEHIND you suddenly pops up BEFORE you.

Getting Past My Past: In the gospel of John 5, we encounter a crippled man stuck on the same mat for the last thirty-eight years at a place in Jerusalem called the Pool of Bethsaida. We sit front and center to watch Jesus restore the posture of this paralytic back to his upright position.

What a beautiful moment when the omnipotent Savior heals this impotent stranger!

But there's more happening in this passage than what meets our first glance. There is another miracle that transpires in this story that could easily be overlooked.

The first miracle involves the healing of the man's crippling infirmity; the second miracle entails the redemption of the man's painful history.

In John 5:8, Jesus Christ commands the man, "Pick up your mat and walk!" When you think about what the "mat" signifies in this story, it makes you scratch your head and wonder why Jesus ordered him to pick it up. For the man, the mat was a painful reminder of his past. The mat signified the setting in which he stayed stuck for thirty-eight years. To bring this close to home, Jesus ordering the man to pick up his mat is like Jesus instructing you to carry all of the painful emblems of your past. Imagine if Jesus asked you to carry around those sad photographs of yourself as a child. Envision Jesus asking you to lug around the stick your mother or father used to beat you, or the underwear stained with blood after you were violated, or the mug shots the police took after you were arrested. Why would Jesus ask you to pick up the emblems of your painful past and carry them with you?

What do you do with your mat? What do you with all of those painful tokens of your past? There are three particular options before you to manage the memories of yesteryear. The first two options are what you're probably prone to do; the last option is what Jesus asks you to do.

1. Lose it!

To *lose* your mat means that you move forward with life and pretend that your past does not exist. You leave your mat on the sidewalk behind you. You advance onward with grit, wit and staying fit. When your spouse asks you questions about your childhood, you deflect the conversation by saying something like, "So, how about them Yankees?" When certain people from yesteryear hit you up on your cellphone, you send their call to voicemail. You would rather not be reminded of where you came from. You have your own way of putting all of those painful experiences in the rear, hoping that they never reappear again. You pressed your foot against the gas, driving 100 miles per hour, all to lose your past!

But have you truly moved beyond what's behind you? According to data from over 17,000 patients in Kaiser Permanente's Adverse Childhood study, there's a clear correlation between unresolved trauma and addiction. (The data revealed that individuals who suffered trauma are five times more likely to become alcoholics, sixty percent more likely to become obese and forty-six times more likely to become an injection-drug users. Trauma produces such high levels of cortisol (stress hormone) that you rely on the substance to suppress the stress. In summary, have you surmounted your past or have you just suppressed it?

Agriculture teaches us when you bury a seed, it only appears to have gone away. What truly happens to the seed is that it morphs into something else—something far more prolific than how it started—and reappears in another form at another time. In the same manner, when you bury your past, it only seems to have gone away. The seeds of pain you bury today will blossom into crops of anger, depression, addiction and other harmful vices that reappear on another day.

Jesus never commanded the man to lose his mat. Neither does Jesus encourage you to lose your mat, a.k.a. your past. Coping mechanisms such as denial, suppression or addiction were not tactics listed in the playbook of the Savior. None of these coping mechanisms enable you to escape your past; they only bury your history to resurface as something else at a future date. Usually, whatever you bury crops up at a later time, even stronger. Running from your past is foolish because...

Whatever you run from will run you!

Instead of ordering the man to lose his mat, Jesus instructed him to pick up his mat and walk. In the same manner, Jesus tells you to pick up your past and walk. In handling your history, losing it is not the solution!

2. Choose it!

To *choose* your mat means you stay stuck in the same place you've been your entire life. You surrender to the helpless and hopeless mindset that says, "What was shall always be."

Like the invalid in the story, you stay put in one spot for thirty-eight years in a state of paralysis that denies you access to new opportunities.

When you choose your mat, you resolve that although your pain is unbearable, it's at least predictable. In other words, the devil you know is better than the devil you don't know.

When you choose your mat, you become one of the overwhelming statistics of folks who can't get past their past.

According to research, past behavior is the greatest predictor of future behavior.

According to the research, what a person did is the most accurate forecast of what a person will do.

Or to put it in the words of William Shakespeare, "What's past is prologue."

Check out these alarming statistics that clearly substantiate this claim:

—People who cheated are three-and-a-half times more likely than people who never cheated, to cheat again.

—Sixty-seven percent of people who divorce will divorce again.

—Seventy-six percent of prisoners will be rearrested within five years.

—Eighty-five percent of addicts relapse within five years.

—Fifty percent of people who suffered from depression will suffer again.

—Out of the fourteen contestants from the Biggest Loser reality show, all but one regained their weight within six years.

When you choose your mat, you make the easiest, most typical, decision.

There's no denying the fact that the human specimen is a creature of habit that cannot get out of its own way. Habits are very much like comfortable beds; easy to fall into, but nearly impossible to crawl out of.

Chances are, without supernatural intervention along with some determination on your part, you will choose your mat. Sad to say but most people do what they always did, good, bad or indifferent.

Jesus never commanded the man to choose his mat. He never said to him, "Just sit there at the pool, and do what you always did!" Nope. Instead, he lovingly refuses to leave the paralytic in the condition he found him.

Likewise, Jesus is not telling you to resign yourself to the horrific conditions that have resulted from your past.

He does not say "Lose your Mat!" Nor does he say, "Chose your Mat!" Instead, he says, "Pick up your mat and walk."

3. Use it!

Jesus' instruction to "pick up the mat" insinuates that it has some purpose to serve in this man's present and future. For what reason would Jesus command this man to own his mat if it had no value in his life? Perhaps the value of the mat is that it reminded him of where he came from, keeping him humble throughout his days. Maybe the significance of the mat is that it's a teaching tool that enlightens him about the principles of faith needed for future challenges? Or, perhaps the mat was the evidence to unbelieving onlookers that the man was miraculously healed from a grave ailment? More than likely, the mat accomplished all of these purposes. In short, the man's painful past had tremendous value, or the Savior would have never told him to take it with him. It was an asset that served him rather than a liability that stumbled him. Rather than commanding the man to lose the mat, or choose the mat, Jesus asks the man to *use* the mat.

Likewise, your painful past is not something you should *lose* or *choose* but is something you should *use*. It plays a pivotal role in the journey you walk. Allow me to take a step further and say that your story will prove to be either the greatest asset or liability you own in this life. Your story—all of the horrific events you endured—will become the utmost stepping stone or stumbling block in your journey.

Depending upon how you frame your past,
it will either be an anchor that drags you downward,
or, it will be a rudder that guides you forward.

You choose. If you read the biographies of some of history's most notable heroes and villains, you will discover many parallels between their lives. You will see that both the champions and scoundrels were pulverized by life circumstances from the days of their youth.

For instance, both Charles Manson and Winton Churchill were abandoned by their parents, yet one became *bitter* while the other got *better.* The difference between the heroes and villains has nothing to do with what they went through, but everything to do with what went through them. Here's the bottom line: when you frame your past rightly, you will experience a fulfilling present reality.

Do you know how to SEE and SAY your story?

Let's take another look at your past, only from a different angle than perhaps what you are accustomed to. Often times, beholding something from another angle reveals what we didn't notice initially.

SOCIAL MEDIA EXERCISE: Post on the *Pain Into Parables Facebook Group Page* a picture of yourself reading this book in a sentimental location. Please display the cover of the book in the picture along with elaborating on the significance of the location. Also, please add, #PainIntoParables, at the conclusion of your post.

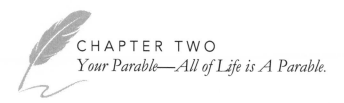

CHAPTER TWO
Your Parable—All of Life is A Parable.

All throughout history, the sages of the ages utilized the literary genre known as parable to enlighten their students about life. In Christianity, Islam and a host of other religions, teachers recited parables to impart wisdom within their pupils about how to behave and what to believe. A parable is a short story, drawing from the situations of life, that illustrates a universal, life-changing truth.

May I submit to you that all of life is a parable—a story that utilizes your circumstances, good and bad, to teach you about deeper things? If you suffered through the loss of someone special, you learned facets of love that romance novels cannot teach. If you endured the heartache of betrayal, you were educated in subjects such as human nature, forgiveness, and trust. If you withstood the shame of being abused, you were schooled in the subjects of resilience, identity, and self-respect.

Hidden within all of life's MESSES is a MESSAGE.

To those with ears to hear, life offers a series of parables that make you smarter, stronger, and sweeter. It's time to pay better attention. In the words of Socrates, "The unexamined life is not worth living." By embracing this mentality, every traumatic experience has the potential of transfiguring you into a victor rather than a victim. By adopting this outlook, all hardships shape you into someone *better* rather than someone *bitter*.

For years, psychologists have conducted studies on post-traumatic stress, a disorder that comes from having your safe, seemingly secure life rocked by the turbulence of pain. Back in the 1990s, two psychologists from the University of North Carolina at Charlotte, Richard G. Tedeschi and Lawrence G. Calhoun, conceptualized *Post-Traumatic Growth*, a theory that adversity is an opportunity to develop higher levels of functioning. The research shows that anywhere between 30-70% of people testify to traumatic experiences being a catalyst for personal growth. That begs the question, what are the people who get *better* doing differently from those who get *bitter*?

Narrative Therapy.

Listen to the manner in which emotionally unstable people describe their past. They say things like, "I wasted twenty years in that marriage!" or "I've been stepped on my whole life!" or "If it weren't for bad luck in my past, I would have had no luck at all!" Now, listen to the way that well-adjusted people elaborate on their yesterdays. They say things like, "I had some troubles but I learned so much!" or "It was difficult, but God got me through!" or "I had some clouds, but thank God for each rainbow the clouds ushered in!" I'll bet you have plenty of anecdotal evidence to show that emotional wellbeing hinges on how you interpret the past.

According to Dr. James W. Pennebaker in his book entitled *Writing to Heal*, substantial research suggests that people who can make meaning out of their messes recover from traumatic experiences better than those who leave it in a muddle. The task of making meaning could include penning our pain into words that capture what we learned from our heartaches.

The theory of counseling that epitomizes what *Pen your Pain into Parables* is all about is known as Narrative Therapy. Developed by social workers Michael White and David Epston in the 1970s, Narrative Therapy encourages people to rewrite their historical narrative by taking a look at the skills and values they learned along their journey. The rewriting of your narrative does not mean altering the facts of whatever happened to you. That kind of rewriting classifies as denial. But the rewriting entails changing your perspective of what happened to you. Rather than getting stuck on what happened to you, ask yourself what values, skills, or lessons were acquired from such an ordeal. In order to pen your pain into a parable, you should ask yourself the questions:

1. How has my pain made me SMARTER?

When you pen your pain into parables, one of the first questions to ask yourself, "How has my pain made me smarter?" or "What lessons did I learn from the ordeals I endured?" For instance, perhaps you were taught about the consequences of hanging out with the wrong company. In the words of my pastor, "If you hang around with dogs long enough, you will soon catch fleas." Or, maybe you were enlightened about the sufficiency of God when all you had was a wing and a prayer. In the words of Mother Theresa, "You don't know God is all you need, until God is all you have." These are the lessons learned by those who have been through the fire.

Once upon a time, a student inquired of his elder, "How do I become successful?" The elder replied, "Good decisions." A bit perplexed, the student asked, "How do I acquire the wisdom to make good decisions?" The elder settled the matter, "Bad decisions." In summary, *setbacks* that result from bad decisions become *setups* that make us wiser for better decisions. But it all hinges on how you frame your past.

Is your painful past something you despise? Or, do you see your past as a series of lessons that made you wise?

History teaches us that Ludwig Van Beethoven (1770-1827) started losing his hearing at twenty-six years old and went completely deaf by forty-six years old; a fear that ironically tormented him from the days of his youth. Beethoven believed that deafness would plunder from him the pleasure of composing his classical music. To his own surprise, he wrote his last five sonatas and his Ninth Symphony after losing his hearing. Scholars esteem these later works as his finest!

Could it be that Beethoven's miseries are what inspired his melodies? Could it be that the emotional pain is what expanded his brain? Some of the most eloquent poems, inspiring songs, and compelling paintings throughout history were composed by heart-broken composers. In the words of the late Carrie Fisher, "Take your broken heart and make art."

2. How has my pain made me STRONGER?

When you pen your pain into parables, the second question you want to ask yourself is, "How has my pain made me stronger?" For instance, one of my dearest friends was a fledgling, sensitive girl when she married her first love over twenty-five years ago. After suffering through years of verbal abuse, her skin thickened from the continual insults. Of course, she admits she stayed far too long in those circumstances. Nonetheless, the ordeal made her stronger. Some folks might describe her as a "woman with walls" but walls aren't always a bad thing. In ancient times, walls were used to safeguard a city from being attacked by intruders. I would argue that the walls she erected make her the secure woman she is today.

In the Old Testament, an adolescent shepherd named David faces up to a nine-foot giant named Goliath whom he slays with his slingshot. Where did David acquire such vigor to overcome such a behemoth? The answer is he gleaned strength from his past. Notice how he perceives his past in 1 Samuel 17:35-36: "When a lion or bear came and carried off a sheep from the flock, I went out after it, struck it and rescued the sheep from its mouth. When it turned on me, I seized it by its hair, struck it and killed it. Your servant has killed both the lion and the bear. This uncircumcised Philistine will be like one of them."

More than likely, David bore emotional and physical scars from his intense clashes with such beasts; however, the strength he drew from those experiences is what he remembered and applied in his later struggles. When you pen your pain into parables, think carefully on how your narrative of mayhem has made a warrior out of you.

May I submit to you that the reward for every struggle is the strength for the next struggle?

3. How has my pain made me SWEETER?

When you pen your pain into parables, the final question you should ask yourself is, "How has my pain made me sweeter?" When I say "sweet" I'm referring to that empathy and compassion born within the incubator of personal suffering. If you ask compassionate people to tell you their story, you will hear a narrative of heartache from an abusive childhood, a bitter divorce, tragic loss, financial failures, etc. It was their own personal pain that tenderized their hearts towards their neighbors' plight. Imagine how that once lame man from John 5 felt every time he passed by an invalid stuck on his mat begging for change. It is reasonable to infer that he probably reached out with empathy given the fact that he was so familiar with that particular agony.

Neuroscience backs up the fact that personal agony is what cultivates social empathy. According to medical research conducted by Keysers and Valeria Gazzola at the Social Brain Lab, the part of our brain responsible for experiencing personal agony is the same neurological network that enables us to feel empathy. The implications of this research suggest that when you experience personal agony, you are exercising the same muscle needed for empathy. In short, your suffering transforms you into a sweeter person, if you allow it to do so. This neuroscience finding insinuates that...

Personal agony is the incubator for empathy.
The more you agonize, the more you can empathize.

Right now, analyze the kinds of people you feel the most compassionate towards. Are they abused children, battered women, forgotten shut-ins, stigmatized convicts, etc.?

Chances are, you could draw a line between your agony and your empathy.

For instance, my heart breaks for kids caught in the crossfire of a divorce between two angry parents.

Why? Because I was once that kid.

The Bible stands true to modern scientific research when it says, "He comforts us in all our affliction, so that we may be able to comfort those who are in any affliction, with the comfort which we ourselves are comforted by God" (1 Cor 1:4).

A Great Resource.

Don't let anyone tell you different—your past is not something to bury, forget, or simply *get over!* On the contrary, your story is one of the greatest resources you have. Your mat is a reminder of where you came from, all of the lessons you learned, and the catalyst needed to make you a better person.

You overcome the opponents of today by remembering the victories from yesterday. Throughout the saga of time, folks told their stories to instill morals, pass on religious and cultural legacy, and entertain family and friends. Another reason they told their story was to edify themselves mentally, emotionally, and spiritually. The teller of the story derives overcoming-power by the story they tell.

In Revelation 12:11, the Apostle John tells us, "They overcame the devil by the blood of the Lamb and the word of their testimony." That phrase "word of their testimony" is translated in the original Greek as the vocal utterance of their story of redemption.

Know your story. And just as importantly, learn how to *tell* your story. In the next chapter, you shall learn the skills required to pen your deepest pain into transformative parables.

SOCIAL MEDIA EXERCISE: Post on the *Pain Into Parables Facebook Group Page* a meme that captures one of the lessons you have learned in life. Also, please add, #PainIntoParables, at the conclusion of your post.

CHAPTER THREE
Your Pen—Finding Your Story

Like archeologists who search through rubbish for a hidden artifact, such is the task of finding your story. In their pursuit, archeologists rummage through ancient wreckage for days and weeks, they dig and dig while knowing something small, yet incredibly valuable, is buried underneath all of the debris. In the same manner, precious artifacts are hidden within the wreckage of your past. These precious articles include truths about God, lessons of life, observations about human nature, discoveries about yourself, etc.

To find your story means to reexamine your past,
and unearth the gems hidden within every painful experience.

In order to find your story, retrospection awaits you. If you ever stood on the balcony of a penthouse, you've beheld a vantage point that affords you the most wide-ranging view of the city. From that belvedere, you notice details you could never see when standing in the middle of the city.

That's retrospection—a vantage-point that offers you a complete, thorough view of your past.

Through retrospection, you see the stuff about God, yourself, and others that you could have never seen while in the middle of your situations. The old Indian adage stands true, "If you want a definition for water, don't ask a fish." A fish is too immersed in its surroundings to define it. It has no counter-perspective. In the same way, you have no counter-perspective of the circumstances of which you are immersed within. You only understand something when you come out of it and look back at it. The Bible promises you that you will gain something valuable from every trial, according to I Peter 5:10, only *after* you have suffered for a while.

Why Write it Down?

Perhaps you are wondering, "Why do I need to write down my story? Why not simply share it in conversation with family, friends and whomever?" Without diminishing the value of vocalizing your story, let me offer you a few reasons from the research on why writing your story is essential.

There is a staggering amount of data that suggests your pen is not just a tool that reveals what you feel; but an apparatus that heals what you feel.

1. Writing has shown to reduce cortisol levels (stress hormone). In one study performed at the University of Chicago, anxious test-takers were less nervous after writing about their thoughts and feelings. Given the fact that many of our past events exacerbated our stress, it would make sense that we engage in a task like writing to alleviate that same stress.

2. Writing has shown to bring cognitive clarity to complexities. According to business tycoon Warren Buffet, writing is a task that enables him to refine his thoughts. Given the fact that many of our past events caused confusion, it would make sense that we engage in a task such as writing that brings clarity.

3. Writing has shown to improve the health of trauma sufferers. In a study conducted by Dr. James W. Pennebaker, forty-six college students were asked to write about traumatic life events or trivial matters for four consecutive days. Six months later, the findings indicated that the students who wrote about their traumas visited the campus health center less frequently, as well as ingesting pain relievers less often, than the students who merely wrote about petty issues.

Tell Your Story.

Using the acronym, P.I.C.T.U.R.E., I offer you a tool that will help you pen your pain into parables. Truth be told, you could embark upon such a journey in multiple ways; however, this tool has proven to be helpful to me and others who have taken my classes. Starting on page 130, you'll find a short workbook where you can make notes. You may also want to consider the specially-formatted workbook that is available online to accompany this book: *Pen Your Pain Into Parables–A Tool for Recovery Workbook*

P – Pain

Begin the process by identifying a *Motif Pain*–a particular hurt that has followed you all throughout your life. Perhaps it's the ache of rejection, abandonment, shame, inadequacy, failure, embarrassment, or any other type of agony. Allow yourself the space to compose all of the related feelings, thoughts, and even physical manifestations that occur as a result of this pain. Or, just write about an emotional pain bothering you in the present. More often than not, what bothers you now has stalked you from the days of your youth; perhaps a different set of circumstances but the same underlying emotions. For instance, I have a friend of twenty years that regularly laments about being overlooked.

One job after another, he shares with me the same feelings of being unnoticed or even snubbed by his supervisors and colleagues. That's his Motif Pain, the feeling that plagued him since he was a kid. The psalmist alludes to this Motif Pain when he says, "My enemies (internal and external) have greatly oppressed me from my youth, but they have not gained the victory over me" (Ps. 129:2).

A Motif Pain is a particular type of pain that has stalked you since your youth.

Trust where your pen guides you. If you start off writing about rejection, but it leads to shame, then go with it. The task of writing leads to self-discovery, shedding light upon various regions of our heart. The task of writing is very much like peeling back an onion; you begin with what's on the surface, and layer by layer, work towards the inner core. It takes some time to get to what's getting at you. King Solomon says, "Counsel in the heart of man is like deep waters, but a man of understanding will draw it out" (Prov. 20:5).

One of the reasons why it takes time to reach the core of our pain is because we tend to avoid uncomfortable feelings. Also, some of us grew up in homes where we were made to feel guilty about what we feel.

You should know that your feelings are not right or wrong; they just are. Pay no mind to those dismissive voices of your past. Instead, trust when your pen guides you to the core of your pain.

The real story is not what you went through, but what went through you.

An explicit description of the people, places, and things surrounding your pain will not result in the breakthrough you need. Freedom emerges when you discuss how these people, places, and things affected you mentally, emotionally, and spiritually. Be willing to look at what lies beneath the exterior. There, you will encounter the damage that's been done, and there you will experience the healing power of God.

Below, you will find a list of various kinds of Motif Pain you might want to explore. More than likely, you will relate to most of the pain on this list. Select one that seems to be a theme in your life.

This is not an exhaustive list but merely scratching the surface of what lies within your heart: *Rejection, Loneliness, Abandonment, Inadequacy, Jealousy, Fear, Regret, Shame, Grief/Loss, Anxiety, Obsession, Frustration, Mistrust, Resentment, Pessimism, Confusion, Paranoia, Gloom Hopelessness, Doubt, Emptiness, Insecurity, Guilt, Despair, Anger, Helplessness, Worry, Dread.*

I – Incident

Think about your life as a movie with a sequence of scenes. Select a particular scene, or *Incident*, that corresponds with your *Motif Pain*. This incident could have occurred anytime in your life prior to the present. The incident does not have to be something catastrophic to be significant. A paper cut can be just as painful to the flesh as being struck with a hammer. The incident can be as minuscule as arriving late for gym class in the fifth grade; if the incident pertains to your Motif Pain, then write about it. The only requirement for the selection of your incident is that the situation be related to your Motif Pain.

For instance, let's assume your Motif Pain is shame. In this case, you might reflect upon showing up at your high school prom with a bulging, shiny pimple on your nose. In this case, you explore the pain of shame within the context of your pimply prom. Resist the temptation to jump around to other scenes in your life; it is better to go deeper with one scene than go broader with a litany of scenes. It is shocking how much one incident—such as the pimply prom—reveals about your pain.

When writing about the incident, think it through with two different lenses. The first lens is called *inspection,* in which you revisit the external details of that scene.

Hark back to the car you drove, the songs played at the prom, the boy or girl you danced with, your hairstyle, your apparel, etc. Scientific research on memory shows that a person vividly dredges up the external elements associated with the pain they felt while discarding other details.

For instance, one study revealed that a victim explicitly remembered the knife used in the attack while she forgot the clothing or vehicle of the attacker. In the pimply prom incident, you might recall a song lyric played at the venue that summarized your feelings while sitting next to your pretty date (e.g., *Beauty and the Beast*) or maybe the tomatoes on your salad that reminded you of the bulge on your nose. No pressure to remember everything; you are not a journalist reporting all of the facts. Instead, pay attention to those details that left an impression on your heart.

The second lens is called *introspection,* in which you recall the feelings and thoughts that passed through you during that incident.

Summon to mind the dread you felt when looking at your pimple in the mirror, the anxiety you experienced when your date arrived, the paranoia of all eyes being on you when you entered the school, etc. Whatever incident you select, bring to remembrance all of the thoughts and feelings that passed through you when standing in the heat of that situation.

When you uncover your story, remember what you went through *(inspection)* as well as what went through you *(introspection)*.

A few caveats about selecting your Incident:

1. The *Fish in Water* tip – Refrain from writing about any ongoing traumatic events. You have to come out of something before you can understand what it's about. As I quoted earlier, "If you want a definition for water, don't ask a fish." A fish has no counter-perspective to understand what envelopes it—it's too immersed in its own situation to understand it.

2. The *Boiling Pot* tip – Abstain from writing about any traumatic event that triggers psychological distress. You will need to see a therapist to talk these issues out before penning them out.

3. The *Let Sleeping Dogs Lie* tip – Do not dig up issues that don't affect you in any way. If the dog is sleeping, let him sleep.

C – *Conflict*

The *Conflict* is the struggle you engage in within your story. Take some time to identify the conflict within the incident you selected. On the surface, the conflict might involve you and another person. Or, it might be between you and some system, like the movie *John Q* where Denzel Washington's character wages war against the medical system. In the case of the pimple, the conflict involves you and your own adolescent biology.

Without conflict, your story is flat; it is the heartbeat of the story that gives it life and keeps it moving. As much as you complain about your conflicts, without them, you would die slowly from agonizing monotony. Conflicts, or challenges, are what makes life energetic and adventurous.

Below the surface, the conflict is always *you* against *you*—a war with your own self-concept, ideas, feelings, fears, etc. Below the surface, it is an internal battle with some underlying issue. The Apostle Paul sheds light on the real conflict we face when he says, "For our struggle is not against flesh and blood, but against the rulers, against the authorities, against the powers of this dark world, and against the spiritual forces of evil in the heavenly realms" (Eph. 6:12). Paul defines the essence of all conflict—a spiritual combat and not a physical one.

For instance, in the movie *Rocky*, the conflict on the surface entails Rocky versus Apollo Creed. Below the surface, the conflict involves Rocky up against his own inadequacy. The feud that Rocky wages with Apollo Creed merely provokes the real battle Rocky faces with his own inner demons.

The real conflict always occurs NOT in the arena of your living room, workplace or church, but within the battlefield of your mind.

The most essential thing to know about conflict is that it serves as the friction God utilizes to shape you. In Proverbs 27:17, King Solomon likens your conflicts to "iron sharpens iron."

The metaphor accentuates how friction sharpens you just as one piece of iron hones another. Your conflicts refine you just like iron sharpens iron. All the arguing you did with your siblings made you smarter. All the fights you engaged in with classmates made you stronger.

As you reflect upon your conflicts, take into account the ways in which they honed your intellect, character and personality.

T – Truth

Now, we come to the touchstone of every parable. Now, we arrive at what distinguishes the parable from other narratives.

A parable is a story about an incident that hinges on a particular *Truth*. It's your job to unearth the precious truth buried within the muck of the incident. When you undertake such a job, it is a prayerful, thoughtful, and soul-searching experience but so worthwhile. When you unearth the truth, it sets you free from particular toxic lies planted within your mind.

Below is a catalogue of four different truths that your incident may have taught you:

A Lesson to Learn.

A teaching you learned, usually through the school of hard-knocks, about life. Something you figured out, typically through feeling the heat rather than seeing the light, about living in this world. For instance, in the parable of the feast in Luke 14, Jesus teaches us that you will be humiliated when you exalt yourself.

A Principle to Practice.

A practical guideline you apply in life in order to reap a certain kind of success. For instance, in the parable of the unjust judge in Luke 18, Jesus teaches us about the principle of persistent prayer and how it pays off.

A Characteristic to Emulate.

An honorable trait that someone exhibits and becomes a virtue to aspire after, such as an admirable attribute that reflects the character of God. For instance, in the parable of the Prodigal Son in Luke 15, Jesus illustrates the merciful love of God, through the characteristics of the father; a love that does not treat someone according to their sins.

An Observation to Remember.

Data acquired about human or divine nature that tempers

your future expectations. For instance, in the parable of the two sons in Matthew 21, Jesus teaches us that a person should not be trusted based on their talk but only on how they walk.

Once you dig up the truth from your past experience, state that truth in a brief, catchy manner with no more than two sentences.

Avoid using cliché statements such as "The early bird catches the worm." Or "Let go and let God."

Try your best to convey that truth in a fresh, original manner. Also, it is effective to wrap up the parable with stating that truth in the last sentence.

U – *Unfolding Action*

The *Unfolding Action* refers to the development of the story's tension from the beginning of the incident to its end. The unfolding action consists of three things, all of which are described below:

Inciting Moment.

This is the small or big event in the beginning of the story that sets off the conflict. For instance, in the story about the pimply prom, the inciting moment could be the instant you noticed the colossal pimple on your nose while staring into your bathroom mirror.

Rising Action.

This refers to the sequence of personal decisions and external happenings, all of which increase the tension of the story. In the pimply prom story, the rising action could be all of your decisions to cure or hide the pimple which only make it worse.

Climax.

This refers to the most intense part of the story, and it's turning point. In the pimply prom story, the climax could be the moment your date insists upon kissing you, giving her a close view of Mount Everest. It's also the moment you decide to not hold back but kiss her back.

The *Unfolding Action* is the buildup of tension that brought you to your breakdown; the moment right before your breakthrough.

R – Resolution

In recovery from traumatic events, closure is something we seek. Closure is defined as "a sense of acceptance that enables us to let go of what was in order to embrace what is." Perhaps we expect closure to come from an apology from someone who wounded us. Maybe we anticipate closure coming from justice of some form for crimes committed against us. We hope for these forms of closure to grease the palms that will not let go of yesterday's tragedies.

But what happens when your offender will not apologize? What happens when the jury finds your abuser, *Not Guilty?* What happens when nobody will validate your grievances? The problem with waiting for closure to happen to us is that it may never happen. Waiting for closure to happen to us could leave us trapped in a cycle of victimization forever.

True closure is not what happens TO you,
but what happens THROUGH you.

Haven't you noticed that the author has the final say-so in every story? Even the most powerful characters cannot usurp the power of the author's pen. Under the inspiration of God, you are the author of your story. The people in your life are merely the characters. You decide how the story will end. You determine if your tale will culminate in tragedy or victory. In many stories, the antagonist refuses to change. In many stories, the antagonist continues to wreak havoc in the lives of people. Fortunately, it is not a change in the antagonist's behavior that guarantees a promising *resolution*. It is the pen of the author that wraps up all loose ends within the story, bringing resolution to the main character, regardless of what happens with the antagonist.

The resolution is the moment of closure that wraps up all loose ends within your parable. It occurs after the climax and leads to the truth of your parable. In the pimply prom story, the resolution might entail your date complimenting you for your kindness—a moment that alleviates tension about your physical appearance and leads to the truth "beauty glows from within."
Select a resolution for your parable; a moment you remember that wrapped up all loose ends within your incident. Select a moment that led to your truth, just as the compliment in the pimply prom story led to the truth about beauty. Keep in mind that the moment does not have to be larger than life; the best stories consists of subtle, simple instances that awaken our souls.

Also, you may not find your resolution within the selected incident. Your resolution might come years later in another scenario related to the incident. That's okay. Sometimes, it requires years of learning for us to understand what the Spirit is saying to us (read my parable called *Loss* in *Chapter Four* as an example of this delayed resolution).

E – Empathy

Empathy is defined as seeing with another person's eyes, thinking with another person's mind, and feeling with another person's heart. According to neuroscience, there resides eleven empathic circuits in the brain that enable us to empathize; sadly, some people's empathic circuits short-circuited at some point during life. Empathy allows you as the writer to take into account the perspectives of others within your story. This empathy supplants all narrow, judgmental thinking. When you write, show empathy towards your younger self, your opponents, your authorities, and whoever else will play a role in your story. Empathizing with the characters of your story will add depth and dimension by showing multiple perspectives.

Also, one of the benefits of empathy is that it helps you forgive the people who hurt you by understanding their handicaps. Chances are, it would be easy to pardon a blind person who knocked over a vase in your house because you understand their limitations. Likewise, the people who injured you are handicapped in some fashion; perhaps limited in the areas of love, respect, or consideration. Empathizing with their handicaps, through your writing, makes forgiveness more bearable. This simply means shedding light on their struggles, or giving them a voice, in your story. Keep in mind, *EMPATHY does not excuse bad behavior, but explains it.*

Lastly, it benefits you tremendously to empathize with God. When you catch His divine perspective, it keeps you from getting stuck in one isolated moment. Instead, His viewpoint enables you to behold a bigger picture. When you gaze at the earth's landscape from an airplane, you do not get overwhelmed by the graffiti on a sidewalk or the bad paint-job on a house; instead, a view of the big picture takes your breath away. Likewise, perceiving your past through divine lens allows you to see how God weaves all of your moments together into one beautiful tapestry. As the scripture says, "And we know that in all things God works for the good of those who love him, who have been called according to His purpose" (Rom. 8:28).

This kind of empathy becomes obtainable when you pray

(which opens your spirit), read the sacred scriptures (which opens your mind), and engage in relationship with other believers (which opens your heart). Incorporate this kind of empathy within your story by expounding upon the manner in which God weaved your pain into His purposes.

Your Voice.

Your *voice* is the unique perspective through which you communicate your story. For instance, you may have a poetic voice, utilizing lots of metaphors and figures of speech to tell your story. Or, you may have a street voice, speaking in a matter of fact, sarcastic and intuitive style to communicate your message. Or, you may have a philosophical tone, saturated with abstract language, that couches your story in some loftier context. Or, you may have an introspective tone, revealing lots about your own thoughts and feelings. Of course, you could have a mix of any one of these styles along with a litany of unmentioned others.

Also, another aspect of your voice pertains to the tense you use. You may tell your story with present tense verbs, as if it's happening in the here and now. This tense allows the reader to walk through your story in real time, creating an impactful experience. This tense also allows you to relive the emotions you experienced during that incident. Or, you may tell your story in the past tense, looking back at it from a distance. If you haven't healed from the pain of that incident, it may be better to use the past tense.

Lastly, another aspect of your voice pertains to whether you write in first-person point of view or third-person point of view (second-person point of view is not recommended). When you write with a first-person point of view, you employ the pronouns, *I, Me and My,* when referring to yourself. When you write in the first-person point of view, it allows you to be transparent about what you think and feel in your writing. When you write with a third-person point of view, you employ the pronouns *He or She* when referring to yourself. The benefits of the third-person point of view is that it allows you some emotional distance from the pain of the moment you are capturing. If you are still raw over what happened, it is recommended that you write with a third-person point of view.

From a Traumatized Mind to Triumphant Mind

When God designed our brains, He hard-wired the organ with malleable material. Fortunately, much like a piece of clay, the brain possesses the inherent capacity to be shaped and reshaped even after its been molded into the most deplorable design. In light of this scientific fact, even the most fractured brains can be restored. Below, you will discover three particular ways that penning your pain into parables transforms the traumatized mind into a triumphant mind.

1. Wholeness

In the King James rendition of John 5:6, Jesus asks the invalid if he wants to be *whole*. The term, *whole,* means to be fully integrated, having all your faculties working together in unison. Imagine an on automobile in which all of the parts under the hood are properly aligned with one another. Now, envision what happens with an automobile when the engine and transmission aren't connected properly. Depending upon where the disconnect lies, the car will either malfunction or not function at all. For both minds and machines, the importance of integration cannot be overstated. Let's see what this looks like from a scientific perspective.

One of the most devastating effects of trauma upon the brain is a disconnect between the amygdala (the seat of your emotions) and the prefrontal cortex (the habitat of your thoughts). As a result of this disconnect, traumatized people either feel too much without solid reasoning to regulate their emotions, or don't feel much of anything at all known as numbing. One of the benefits of penning your pain into parables is that the task of narrative writing bridges a gap between your emotions and thoughts. Stepping into any story, especially your own, activates both parts of your brain simultaneously. Thus, we are made *whole* through the story we tell.

2. Calmness

When trauma is stored in the brain, it is not stored in a contextual format with all the right facts; rather, it is filed away in fragments of smells, sounds, sights and sensations.

One of the problems of something being fragmented, or removed from its context, is that it often becomes a larger than life image that terrorizes our minds. For instance, if you were attacked, you might be haunted by close-ups of the blade, or maybe the smell of nicotine on your attacker's coat. These recollections become so huge when removed from their original scenery much like an object when you focus the camera lens on it while blocking everything else.

One of the benefits of penning your pain into parables is that it puts the traumatic incident back in context, where it assumes a smaller size in a much bigger picture. Thus, our troubled minds are calmed by the more completed story we tell.

3. Oneness

Perhaps the greatest consequence of trauma is it undermines our trust in God and Neighbor, thus creating schisms within the most important relationships in our life. Whether betrayed, abused or neglected, our trust is damaged to the point where we withdraw from those we desperately need for survival. Traumatized people often fall prey to the temptation of isolation warned about in Genesis 2:18 where God says, "It is not good for man to be alone".

Another benefit of penning your pain into parables is that it puts us back in touch with the people of our story. This kind of writing awakens our empathy, which enables us to see the world through other's eyes. The resultant empathy paves the way for reintegration into community where we become one with those whom we formerly estranged from. Also, when we share our parables, if we feel comfortable enough, it awakens empathy in others who listen.

SOCIAL MEDIA EXERCISE: Post on the *Pain Into Parables Facebook Group Page* a picture of someone from your past who exhibited the characteristics of Christ. Please share on what they taught you. Also, please add, #PainIntoParables, at the conclusion of your post.

CHAPTER FOUR
Penning My Parables Into Parables

In this chapter, I invite you to enter my private world, access to my own painful moments ranging from subtle discomfort, to moderate distress, to deep agony. More importantly, you can see how I penned my life into parables as I utilized the P.I.C.T.U.R.E formula to frame my painful moments into valuable resources. Also, I provided biblical verses that correlate to the truths I unearthed within these painful moments. For me personally, what God revealed through these moments fits into the larger context of His word.

This chapter offers you a tutorial on how to access your own pain, and translate that pain into parables. It has been said that the best teachers do not tell you what to do, but show you how to do it, and inspire you in the process.

My hope is that this chapter will show you how to pen your own pain into parables as well as inspire you with my own stories. May this chapter equip you with the tools to see and say your own story.

You have a story too; a narrative saturated with lessons to learn, principles to practice, characteristics to emulate, and observations to remember.

Perhaps folks repeatedly told you to leave your mat behind. Maybe family and friends repetitiously warned you to forget what lies behind you. Yet, every attempt to run from your past has resulted in being hunted down by it. Today, try a different approach, a counter-intuitive idea that Jesus himself submits to you. Pick up your mat, own your story, and follow Him into a wonderful destiny that builds off of your painful history. Pen your pain into parables.

In the following section, I provide you with my application of the P.I.C.T.U.R.E formula as well as the final product, the parable. Within the application of the P.I.C.T.U.R.E. formula, you will read my shorthand notes that helped me compose my parables. My hope is for you to learn from these templates so that you can craft your own story as well. Don't let anyone tell you any different. Your story is worth remembering and reciting.

"Pick up your mat and walk" (John 5:8).
Take a P.I.C.T.U.R.E. of Shame

P - *Pain*

The irrational shame of being human. The ludicrous embarrassment over defects that are common to mankind. A feeling of disgrace that stalked me into my adult years. A feeling of freakishness about my humanity.

I - *Incident*

A moment from my early childhood when I visited Cape Cod with my family, and my Papa insisted upon me accompanying him to Dunkin' Donuts without waiting for me to dress. I felt humiliated walking with him in my underwear.

C - *Conflict*

A conflict with public opinion. A conflict with my petite body, mainly my belly-button. Underneath that, a battle with my own delusional shame. I say *delusional* because there's no reason to be ashamed over having a belly-button.

T - Truth

The observation that shame comes from outside sources. The Christ-like characteristic of my Papa, who divulged his own humanity in order to make me feel less freakish about mine.

U - Unfolding Action

Inciting Moment: Stepping outside with my underwear on. Rising Action: Hiding behind dumpster, papa enters Dunkin' Donuts. Climax: Papa takes his shirt off.

R - Resolution

The imagery of papa walking with me back to the hotel with his shirt off. The feelings of shame diminishing because of Papa's gesture of kindness.

E - Empathy

Looking at the world through the eyes of a little kid (myself) who felt ashamed along with Papa's compassionate perspective.

A Parable on Shame

Looking down at my belly-button, what I notice is a grotesque hole within my flesh that should be plugged with something like a cotton-ball...immediately! In reality, my belly-button is not unlike that of any other five-year-old boy—a teeny, deep puncture above my groin with an occasional lint inside of it from whatever shirt I wear. But being a boy who easily blushes, that same body part appears so hideous that it must be hidden. I take cover behind a Dunkin' Donuts dumpster as my Papa Tony stepped inside to purchase coffee and muffins for our family. I would have worn a t-shirt like every other tourist gallivanting across Cape Cod, but Papa was too impatient for me to dress. So, here I am, a five-year old boy hiding the shocking reality that

I have a belly-button. Shame is a distorted self-awareness that causes you to feel like a freak about the stuff that merely makes you human.

Maybe I would not feel this way about my bare torso had I not been teased by a relative a few days prior. *"Put some meat on that body, boy! You look like a meatless skeleton."* Crouching behind the putrid trash container, hoping nobody notices me as I pray for Papa to hurry along, I reminisce on an earlier era when I sprinted across the ocean-shore shirtless and shameless, quite possibly unaware that I even had a belly-button. After being called meatless, my belly-button contorted in my mind as one of the great eyesores of civilization. Shame is not something that crops up from inside, but comes to you from outside sources. Hence, the reason God quizzes Adam and Eve as they hid from His presence, "Who told you that you were naked?"

Exiting the Dunkin' Donuts with coffee at hand, Papa discerns instantly I am out of sorts. Perhaps the sight of me tiptoeing on the sly back into public view, from behind the dumpster, reveals everything he needs to know about my frame of mind. Papa places the coffee and muffins down on a nearby table, removes his own t-shirt and drapes it around his waist.

Hand in hand, an old European immigrant strolls with a young lad back to their beachside motel while the sun beats against their naked torsos. Next to papa, all blushing ceases. Shame's survival rate diminishes when you find someone willing to show you that they have a belly-button too.

Key Bible Verse:

God said: "Who told you that you were naked? Have you eaten from the tree that I commanded you not to eat from?" (Gen. 3:11).

"Pick up your mat and walk" (John 5:8).
Take a P.I.C.T.U.R.E of Daddy Issues

P - *Pain*

All of the confusion and uneasy feelings that come from an estranged relationship with my father due to a strife between him and my mother.

I - *Incident*

A moment when my father showed up on Christmas Eve, pounding on our apartment door, after my mother filed a restraining order against him. A moment when my mother called the police and was surprised by what she saw when they asked her to open the door.

C - *Conflict*

A conflict between my father and mother in which my heart was jammed in the middle. Underneath it all, my own internal battle with conflicting perceptions of my father.

T - *Truth*

The characteristics of love being brave, generous and relentless.

U - *Unfolding Action*

Inciting Moment: My father pounding on the door. Rising Action: Mom threatening to call cops, then calling. Climax: Cops asking mom to open door.

R – *Resolution*

The instant my mother sees the hallway crammed with toys. The realization that my father loved me relentlessly.

E - *Empathy*

Looking at the world through the eyes of a fearful young woman, a desperate young father and a confused child.

A Parable on Daddy Issues

When I was too young to comprehend the necessity of boundaries, my mother filed for a restraining order against my father. In his defense, he never laid a malicious hand on his hot tamale wife or his adored children.

Despite his gonzo reputation on the streets, he play-wrestled with me on the bed, often boosting my ego by letting me pin him down Hulk Hogan style while I beat my little chest. Yet, mom filed for reasons that my peanut-sized brain couldn't fathom. Years later, I figured out that boundaries are essential, not merely for physical protection, but for guarding the most fragile parts of who we are, the mind and the heart.

All I recall from that Frank Capra colored evening with a Jerry Springer twist, just a few nights before Christmas, was the incessant pounding on the apartment door. "Cappy (Dad's nickname), go away or I'm calling the police," she reluctantly said. It would not be the first friendly visit the boys in blue paid; a couple of years prior, they busted into the apartment with their guns blazing on the hunt for Dad. But Dad didn't care.

When the police arrived, before they enforced his exodus, the officer said to my mother who poked her nose through a cracked-open door, "Ma'am, you might want to come out into the hallway for a moment before we make him leave." It was a strange request that probably made her feel uneasy, but she trusted the uniform enough to submit to his request.

Opening the door without opening her heart, she stepped into that housing project hallway to find an unusual sight, a corridor crammed with so many Christmas presents that it looked like an aisle from Toys R Us.

While the laws of the land enforce boundaries between individuals, love itself is an impossible thing to restrain.

Key Bible Verse:

"Love never fails" (1 Cor. 13:8).

"Pick up your mat and walk" *(John 5:8).*

Take a P.I.C.T.U.R.E. of People-Pleasing

P - *Pain*

The pain of being taken advantage of by others. The emotional load of carrying another's issues. The mental weight that comes from assuming full responsibility for other's problems. It is a pain that started in early childhood, followed me into the ministry, and still haunts me today.

I - *Incident*

A moment from the fourth grade when classmates preyed upon my people-pleasing nature. A moment when my friends took advantage of my *go along to get along* personality. It was a moment that left me feeling resentful and perturbed with myself for missing out on an opportunity.

C - *Conflict*

A conflict with classmates. A conflict with time. The bell ringing and my wishes to get back to class first. Underneath that, a battle with my own people-pleasing tendencies.

T - *Truth*

The lesson that every person is responsible for taking out their own trash. The principle that I should refrain from taking responsibility for what's not mine.

U - *Unfolding Action*

Inciting Moment: I take my friend's empty candy bar

wrapping. Rising Action: The bell rings while I walk in the opposite direction to dump the trash. Climax: I miss the opportunity to select the story I want to read.

R - *Resolution*

The realization that it was my people-pleasing issue that caused me to forego an opportunity for myself.

E - *Empathy*

Looking at the world through the eyes of a little kid (myself) who just wants to help his friends.

A Parable on People-Pleasing

"Michael, hold this for one second please," my buddy insists while handing over his Snickers. "Sure thing," I respond accommodatingly. Examining the candy bar a bit closer, I detect there's nothing left of the delicacy but a caramel-stained wrapper. Further away into the schoolyard, just beyond the trash barrel, I spot my buddy chuckling with the other kids looking back at me. It's one of those typical fourth grade games where the kids pick on the buffoon of the bunch. This is not the first time he hoodwinked me into taking ownership of his trash. I'm always an easy-mark, because I am the simpleton who *goes along to get along.*

Moseying towards the trash barrel to discard the plastic wrapper, I hear the school bell chime and the kids sprint back towards class. Twenty minutes before recess began, Mrs. Fields had announced that the kid who arrives back the earliest gets the opportunity to select this afternoon's storybook. I would outrun everyone back to class so we could listen to Mrs. Fields mimic Aslan's doting voice while reciting *The Lion, the Witch and the Wardrobe.* But when the school bell chimed, I am strolling south towards the trash barrel while my classmates dash north towards the prize. This was a habit that would haunt me for years to follow: I forego wonderful opportunities for myself because I am too preoccupied with taking out another's trash.

Returning to class about forty seconds later than everyone else, I hear Mrs. Fields reading a book by Judy Bloom, a tale I consider puddle-deep in comparison to the intellectual profundity of CS Lewis. "Shucks! I missed my chance!" I fume. My buddy pivots his head towards me and impishly grins while listening to the storybook of his selection. Resentment bubbles up within me like a shaken soda-bottle just before opening the cap. I think about how many times I've been beaten because I *go along to get along*. It would take another several decades for me to realize a truth that would spare me a great deal of unnecessary grief. If it's not yours, don't pick it up.

Key Bible Verse:
"For each one should carry their own load" (Gal. 6:5).

"Pick up your mat and walk" (John 5:8).
Take a P.I.C.T.U.R.E. of Fear

P - Pain

A fear that arouses the imagination, instigates wild speculations and magnifies the presence of evil within our minds.

I - Incident

A time during my young adulthood when I came face to face with a bad man from my childhood. Welcoming the visitors of our church on a Sunday morning from the pulpit, I realize that one of the visitors is the man who murdered my father's best friend.

C - Conflict

A conflict with the "boogey man." Underneath it, a battle with fear itself.

T - Truth

The observation that evil is not as menacing in reality as it manifests in your mind. The principle of facing your fears.

U - Unfolding Action

Inciting Moment: The news of my father's friend being killed by a man named Jerry. Rising Action: The years of dreading Jerry. Climax: My encounter with Jerry from the pulpit during a church service.

R - Resolution

The realization that my father's friend's killer wasn't as intimidating as I envisioned him to be.

E - Empathy

Looking at the world through the eyes of a scared kid.

A Parable on Fear

"Jerry." For most kids in the 1980s, that name signified a cunning mouse that pestered his arch rival, a house-cat named Tom, during an early Saturday morning cartoon.

"Jerry" for me, at the age of six, was the name of the boogey man. He was a renowned gangster answerable for the slaying and dismembering of my father's best-friend.

I never met Jerry in person, nor had I seen his mug on television. My father would shut off the T.V. at the onset of the news broadcast before I had the chance to see the monster.

Yet, the mere whisper of his name roused my gullible mind with haunting images of a ghoulish fella with blood-soaked fangs and razor-sharp fingernails.

Night after night, I twitched in my sleep under the dread of him breaking into our apartment to finish off all of my father's affiliates. Fear feeds off of the element of the unknown, fueled by what might be rather than what is.

The last time I saw my father's slain friend Vin, my teeny legs draped over his shoulders while he paraded me through the Midland Mall. Vin was a hip dude, he was Hollywood enough to charm the loveliest ladies, yet humble enough to roll on the floor with a bratty kid.

I remember feeling a strong connection with him, believing that his coolness could rub off on me, enabling me to allure the pretty redhead seated behind me in my first grade class.

But the day came when Vin was no more.

I wondered if the boogey man who snuffed him out saw me on his shoulders that day in the mall.

I prayed to God that if he showed up in our apartment in the middle of the night, I could thwart him off with the spider-man web I received for Christmas just a few months before.

Over twenty years later, while serving as an associate pastor of a church in Rhode Island, I publicly welcomed the first-time visitors from the pulpit on a Sunday morning.

"What's your name, sir?" I enquired of the sketchy looking fella seated in the third row. "Jerry," he mumbled. And there he was, just a few feet in front of me, the monster who invaded my dreams throughout childhood.

There he was, just a couple seats ahead, the savage murderer of my father's cool friend. He was a small-framed man who wouldn't look me in the eyes.

When you come face to face with your fears, don't expect to be frightened by some larger than life beast. Instead, anticipate the boogey man to be a mere troll.

Key Bible Verse:
"Even though I walk through the darkest valley, I will fear no evil" (Ps. 23:4).

"Pick up your mat and walk" (John 5:8).
Take a P.I.C.T.U.R.E. of Hyper-Vigilance

P - Pain

Mistrust of allowing people into my private world. The anxious anticipation of being hurt by those who attempt to make their way into my life. The hyper-vigilant behaviors that result from this anxiousness. This mistrust was rooted in early incidences where my safety was placed in jeopardy.

I - Incident

A moment from early childhood when I wrongly presumed that our house was being invaded by bad people. A moment when I kept the door of our apartment shut as I saw someone trying to make their way in. A moment that provoked fears that were rooted in earlier moments when my safety was compromised.

C - Conflict

A conflict with an unknown stranger. Underneath that, a battle with my own fears of being hurt or endangered by outsiders.

T - Truth

The observation that hyper-vigilance often derives from early traumas. The observation that hyper-vigilance will deprive you of blessings.

U - Unfolding Action

Inciting Moment: The apartment door-lock opens. Rising Action: I hold door shut while an unknown stranger pushes the door to enter. Climax: My mother reveals that the person on the other side of the door is a friend.

R - Resolution

The imagery of my mother's friend Bobby standing at the doorway with donuts he bought for my mother and me. My mother explaining who Bobby is.

E - Empathy

Looking at the world through the eyes of a little kid who felt scared.

A Parable on Hyper-Vigilance

Sprawled out on our living-room couch watching H.B.O., I'm startled by the rotation of the top-bolt while our grandfather-clock chimes its 3:00 a.m. tune. It is not bizarre for this ten-year-old boy to indulge on Richard Pryor stand-up comedy in the middle of the night. What's unnerving is an intruder unlocking our front door at such an untimely hour while my mother and baby sister slumber. Being that I am now "the man of the house" (the moniker issued to me by my four foot ten, Italian-American, wooden-spoon carrying grandmother after my father went away), I leap off the Chesterfield with the spirit of a red kangaroo protecting its offspring. The foresight of danger calls for swift instincts to override slow logic, or else tragedy befalls the Caparrelli residence.

As I lean my pint-sized torso against that dense door, I wonder who came to pay us such a strange visit. Could it be the police again? They raided the apartment before, even kicking through the bathroom door, with their Glock 22s aimed at my petite skull. Could it be one of the sketchy cats affiliated with one of my many relatives, outlaws who show no regard for locked doors, gates, or fences. Or, could it be the perpetrator of that recent unsolved murder of a young woman in Warwick, Rhode Island? (Later discovered to be local serial killer, Craig Price.) Whomever it is, I anticipate the worst based on lots of anecdotal evidence. Hyper-vigilance is an amplified state of awareness, triggering intense behaviors, shaped by trauma. Hyper-vigilance is like the residual ringing of the eardrums that continues even after the blaring sound disappears.

Losing the struggle against what seems to be some kind of mammoth, I holler for my mother to awake. With the door nearly wide open, a King-Kong arm reaches towards me from the other side. "What the *bleep!* is going on?" my mother bellows out, using her favorite cuss words. "I need help! Somebody is breaking in!" I reply.

I lose my bearings, the door swings open and a plump man wearing an oversized hearing-aid stands at the threshold with a box of Dunkin' Donuts in his hands. "It's my friend, Bobby" my mother exclaims. Bobby was a harmless fella who showed much kindness to our family during some difficult times. The beauty of hyper-vigilance is that it keeps bad guys out; the tragedy is it disbars good guys from coming in.

Key Bible Verse:

"But whoever listens to me will live in safety and will be at ease, without fear of harm" (Prov. 1:33).

"Pick up your mat and walk" (John 5:8).
Take a P.I.C.T.U.R.E. of Humiliation

P - *Pain*

The humiliation of being a welfare case. The feeling of being stigmatized by my classmates for receiving charity. Up until this very day, I feel humiliated by receiving charity of any sort.

I - *Incident*

A moment from junior high school when my mother sent me into a store to ask if they accept food stamps. The humiliation I felt when asking such a question, and the measures I took to not be seen by anyone I knew.

C - *Conflict*

A conflict with public opinion. Underneath it all, a battle with humiliation. I remember during that season of my childhood that I would lie to people, and tell them I was rich. I hid the fact that we were poor, relying on government assistance. I struggled with a need to be perceived as greater than what I was.

T - *Truth*

The observation that, oftentimes, others are in the same boat you are. The principle of humility; swallowing pride in order to receive gracious blessings.

U - *Unfolding Action*

Inciting Moment: Mom telling me to go into store to ask if they accept food stamps. Rising Action: My caution in the store to not be seen by Autumn. Climax: My classmate entering when the clerk broadcasts that I'm on food stamps.

R - *Resolution*

Mom telling me that Autumn is also on food stamps. She gets cheese because she swallowed her pride.

E - Empathy

Looking at the world through the eyes of a little kid ashamed of being on welfare and a mother struggling financially.

A Parable on Humiliation

It is the usual routine. My mother parks our 1983 tan beach-wagon in front of a Providence vender, whips out a Newport 100 cigarette, and asks me to carry out her dirty work. Before she commissions me, I roll up the sleeves of my New York Yankees sweatshirt, prop my chin up like I'm a Roman gladiator and prepare myself to execute the mission. I despise what Mom requires from me, but I smell the extra-sharp provolone cheese from behind the meat counter making it all worthwhile. With her pseudo-sweet tone, she says, "Mikie, go inside and ask if they accept food stamps."

Before I approach the clerk to carry out my mother's dirty work, I meander down a few aisles to see if there's any familiar faces. I look like I'm "casing the joint," but this prep work is necessary to spare myself from the indignity of being seen as a welfare case. Fortunately, I notice only two strangers. I wait for an opportune moment when it's just me and the clerk. At last, there's an opening!

I cautiously inch my way towards the counter while hearing the chime of the front door as a new patron enters. To my shock, Autumn Roberts arrives, the gossipy freckle-faced redhead who sits behind me in class.

"Can I help you?" the clerk inquires. In a sound frequency that only bats could hear, I ask that appalling question. "Speak up, son," the clerk insists. One more time, I make my request known while pleading with God to deafen Autumn for at least ten seconds. "I'm not sure," the clerk says, "This is my first day." Cupping her hands around her mouth to turn it into a bullhorn. "Mr. Samson, this little boy has a question about food stamps," the clerk hollers across the store.

Standing at the crossroad of my pride and provolone cheese, I'm facing two choices. Choice #1: I sprint out of the store to save my pride. Choice #2: Accept the fact that I'm a schmuck, and walk out the store with my cheese. The second option also means that Autumn knows I'm a welfare case, and probably blasts it within the school yard. In that humiliating moment, I learned that the cost attached to receiving something free is the steep expense of ego. I couldn't taste the provolone without being willing to swallow my pride.

"So, what did they say?" my mother asks as I hide in the last row of the wagon. "They don't accept food stamps," I reply. "That's strange because Autumn made her way into the store. Her mom is on food stamps too."

Key Bible Verse:

"God opposes the proud but shows favor to the humble" (1 Pet. 5:5).

"Pick up your mat and walk" (John 5:8).
Take a P.I.C.T.U.R.E. of Loss

P - Pain

The pain of losing people in your life with whom you bond. More in particular, the pain of losing people whom you commiserate with. To this day, I hate saying goodbye to people.

I - Incident

A moment from my elementary school years when I bonded with a girl by hearing and sharing dysfunctional stories of our home life, and the instant she left the school. The pain I felt with saying goodbye to her.

C - Conflict

A conflict with letting go of a girl who said goodbye to me. Underneath it all, a battle with grief.

T - Truth

The observation that pain will draw you close to people who aren't always good company. The lesson of accepting loss as sometimes what God allowed for your own good.

U - Unfolding Action

Inciting Moment: An unlikely friendship sparked. Rising Action: The differences between us becoming apparent. Climax: She says goodbye.

R - Resolution

The imagery of me colliding into her at a gas station, and noticing needle marks on her arms.

E - Empathy

Looking at the world through the eyes of a kid afraid to lose someone, and a troubled girl.

A Parable on Loss

Like Forest and Jennie, we were peas and carrots. Nearly every day, I cozied up next to her during recess and offered her a Funny Bone (a true sacrifice given the fact that I wouldn't even divvy up that chocolate delicacy with my own kinfolk) while we exchanged sob stories about our home lives. She lamented about the agony of living with melancholy Mom since Dad traded her in for a younger model while I vented about our family's most recent encounter with the cops. We were made for one another; that's how I perceived the regular rendezvous with my heartthrob. But what I didn't understand in my thirteen-year-old brain is that affliction is just as powerful of a magnet as affection. Pain works much like an adhesive, binding heartbroken souls together in one accord.

Apart from our mutual sob stories, we did not share much in common. I dreamt about being a prolific author living in a Manhattan brownstone while she envisioned an undisturbed, small-town existence on the countryside. I reached for the stars while she felt settled with her feet on the ground. In the moment I gave her half my Funny Bone, I should have known we were hewn from different rocks. She ate hers nibble by nibble while I inhaled mine in one gulp. Yet, as unalike as we were, our mutual agony blinded me from discerning reality. William Shakespeare nailed it when he said, "Misery acquaints a man with strange bedfellows."

When she said goodbye, it felt like life was over. Her mother received a job opportunity in another state, leaving me feeling forsaken. She gently grasped my hand, smooched me on the cheek (the most action I ever got at that age) and said, "Farewell, my friend."

Many years later, I sadly found out that her pain drove her down a road of addiction while my pain catapulted me into a path marked by ambition. I discovered this reality when I collided into her at a gas station, and noticed needle-marks on her arms. One of the hardest lessons for me to learn was that God unexplainably removes company that will derail your destiny. Some of the best pea dishes cooked up in the kitchen do not include carrots in the recipe.

Key Bible Verse:

"Let's part company. If you go to the left, I'll go to the right; If you go to the right, I'll go to the left" (Gen. 13:9).

"Pick up your mat and walk" (John 5:8).
Take a P.I.C.T.U.R.E of Jealousy

P - Pain

The angst that comes from jealousy, and the underlying fear of being forsaken by someone I love.

I - Incident

A moment from my elementary school years when I learned that my mother favored my best friend over me by allowing him to stay up late beyond curfew. A moment when I felt jealousy towards my best friend, and resentment towards Mom.

C - Conflict

A conflict with my best friend; someone whom I perceived as a threat to my relationship with Mom. Underneath it all, a battle with the fear of being abandoned by Mom.

T - Truth

The observation that jealousy makes enemies out of even friends. The observation that underneath jealousy is a fear of being forsaken.

U - Unfolding Action

Inciting Moment: Overhearing my friend talk about my mother letting him stay up. Rising Action: My cynical view of my buddy. Climax: I leave my buddy to walk home alone.

R - Resolution

The imagery of me walking home, realizing that I'm really scared of being ditched by my mother. The realization that my angst is not related to my buddy and I, but between my mother and I.

E - Empathy

Looking at the world through the eyes of a kid scared to be forsaken by mom.

A Parable on Jealousy

Over the racket of the rubber ball bouncing, my classmates cheering, and the school bell ringing, I somehow overhear my buddy whispering to someone about how my mother allowed him to remain awake until midnight to watch a televised wrestling match. Propping my head above all of the schoolyard commotion, I read the moving of his lips, "Mikie was sleeping. It was past his curfew." Eyeballs east with my head north, I catch him smirk about the privileges afforded to him that were denied to me. As he approaches, he presumes it not possible for me to have overheard his exchange. He looks at me oblivious, like I know nothing about the special bond he shares with my mother...*my* mother, not *his* mother! But he underestimates the power of jealousy, a state of mind that transmutes an average person into an expert-eavesdropper with bionic senses. Little is the likelihood of the best private investigator in the world uncovering more data than what a jealous person digs up.

"Hey Mikie, do you want the other half of my Snickers?" he asks in his pseudo-friendly tone. *What a shallow atonement for betraying our friendship!* I cynically interpret his offering as no different than that slimy Judas turning over the coins to make right his wrongs against the Savior. Instead of receiving his offering, I respond with the *Malocchio* (an Italian superstition known as 'the evil eye'), a glare capable of paralyzing every soul it targets. "Geez, who peed in your Cheerios this morning?" he says while storming off annoyed as I continue to stare him down. Through the lens of jealousy, every close friend mutates into a detested foe.

In the past, we walked home together given the fact that my buddy lived with us since his mom died. But on this awful day, I choose a different route to travel as that his company makes me gag. As I walk towards home, I imagine entering my bedroom to find his Boston Red Sox framed photographs hang where my Michael Jackson poster once lived. I envision seeing his collection of baseball cards stacked on the shelves where my Langston Hughes poetry books stood. I dread hearing my mother's voice yell, "Bobby, is that you sweetie?" as she hears the front door open from her bedroom. For a moment of clarity, I realize these ill-feelings are not about me being inferior to my buddy, but all about me being ditched by my mother. When you unmask jealousy, you may find a fear of being forsaken.

Key Bible Verse:

"Never will I leave you; never will I forsake you" (Heb.13:5).

"Pick up your mat and walk" (John 5:8).
Take a P.I.C.T.U.R.E of Love-Sickness

P - Pain

The spell that comes with falling for someone.

I - Incident

A time when I rode my bicycle miles to a girl's home, only later on to find out that she already had a boyfriend.

C - Conflict

A conflict pertaining to winning the affections of a girl. Underneath it all, a battle with my own vulnerabilities towards the opposite sex.

T - Truth

An observation about the influence of a woman's voice. A lesson about not being so susceptible to a woman's voice.

U - Unfolding Action

Inciting Moment: The girl's invitation to visit her. Rising Action: The struggle to get to her home miles away by bike. Climax: Finding out that she already had a boyfriend.

R - *Resolution*

Throwing my bike away, symbolizing my breaking free from the hold that a girl had on me.

E - *Empathy*

Looking at the world through the eyes of an emotionally vulnerable young boy.

A Parable on Love-Sickness

With a spellbinding tone, she said to me, "It would be nice to see you after school sometime. If you're ever in the neighborhood, stop by to say hello." Aside from her deep-seated, Shirley Temple dimples, spiraling brown hair and eyes like emeralds, it was the sound of her voice that put a spell over me. In a frenzy, I left school, stopped at the nearest gas station, bought a map and calculated the distance between our houses at eight miles. "Eight miles ain't nuttin," I reasoned. For the next several hours, I rode my rickety bicycle up steep hills and over graveled roads, all to find the girl. When I finally reached the end of her street, I used my paisley bandana to swab the perspiration from my face. I saw her in the front yard. With as much poise as I could pretend, I uttered, "I was in the neighborhood and thought I'd stop by to say hello."

"Hey, it's you again," she replied with her hypnotic tone. Dazzled by my darling, I could not say much other than something stupid like, "Yeah, you like my bike?" Facts were, my bike looked like it was bought discounted at a yard sale in the projects; it was nothing to boast about. "You're an idiot," I thought, "now, you have to redeem yourself." Regrettably, her father called her into the house before I could salvage my image; maybe he called her in for dinner, perhaps to protect her from the deranged little boy on the rickety bike outside his home. I rode eight miles over the course of several hours, all to catch a one-minute glimpse of her. Was it worth it? Heck yea! Riding home, it dawned on me that there were fewer things in this life that could make or break a man's spirit like a woman's voice. What inspired Rocky to return to the ring after hanging his gloves up? Adriane, leaning into his ear, whispered, "Rocky, win!" And what influenced Adam to bite into the fruit, according to God in Genesis 3? "You listened to the voice of that woman."

A few weeks later, I bumped into my darling at a Halloween party. Well, I should say I bumped into her...and him. "Mike, I would like you to meet my boyfriend, Chad," she said brazenly. In reply, I said nothing. Instead, I swallowed real hard, swiftly smiled and walked away. After the party, I went home, took that rickety bike along with the map still sticking out of its half-zippered compartment, and threw it in the trash. I was all done listening to the voice!

Key Bible Verse:

"Because you listened to the voice of your wife" (Gen. 3:17 ESV)

"Pick up your mat and walk" (John 5:8).
Take a P.I.C.T.U.R.E. of Avoidance

P - Pain

The shame that comes from being sexually violated. The pain of not wanting to face the reality of what happened to you.

I - Incident

A time when my mother questioned me about being sexually abused. I jammed my fingers in my ears, avoiding the question. My mother didn't press the issue but served dinner.

C - Conflict

A conflict with my mother over not wanting to discuss a shameful subject. Underneath it all, a conflict with my own shame over what happened.

T - Truth

The characteristic of God (as demonstrated by my mother) in allowing us the time and space to face what ails us; a.k.a. The Patience of God.

U - Unfolding Action

Inciting Moment: My mother asking me about the fondling. Rising Action: All of my avoidant behaviors. Climax: My mother serving dinner.

R - Resolution

Sitting at the dinner table eating as my mother says nothing further. The realization that she handled the situation wisely, knowing that avoidance is sometimes a survival skill.

E - Empathy

Looking at the world through the eyes of an ashamed boy, and an intuitive mom.

A Parable on Avoidance

"I don't want to talk about it!" I snap at her while jamming my pygmy index fingers into my ears. Undeterred by her slow-paced sympathetic tone, I feel like I'm under interrogation for a crime I committed when she poses the question. Even if I'm not *the* culprit, I view myself as somehow complicit for not intercepting the heinous act. As I hear the question, I'm haunted by the words of my first grade teacher, "The doers of evil include those who do nothing about it." That's my self-concept in a nutshell. I'm an evil doer for remaining silent in a moment when I should have protested.

As silly as this sounds, I believe that I can make reality vanish by blocking my senses. My mother asks the question one more time as fingers remain fixed in my ears, "Did Randy touch your *birdie?*" (A term mom used for my penis at six years old.)

For the next twelve years, it is a customary posture I assume when faced with something unpleasant. When my best friend says "goodbye" before moving away to another city, I jam my fingers into my ears. When the teacher warns me that I'm at the cusp of failing geometry, I jam my fingers into my ears. When my first credit card bill arrives in the mail, an expense I cannot afford, I jam my fingers into my ears. Avoidance is a tactic I employ to make troubles evaporate; unfortunately, it causes my troubles to escalate. The grief of a goodbye intensifies from never saying it, the credit card bill compounds with late fees from never paying it, and the shame of being fondled deepens from never confronting it.

After submitting the question a second time, my mother redirects her attention to serving chicken cutlets and mashed potatoes. "Turn off the television. Time for dinner," she says.

When it's not the right time to deal with a particular situation, life must go on in the Caparrelli household. Knowing her, she will contact a clinical professional. For now, I find my seat at the table next to my baby sister's highchair, dip a chunk of chicken into barbecue sauce and notice my mother smiling at me like I'm her treasure. Despite the fact that she's only twenty-two years old, she intuitively knows that avoidance is a tactic needed in certain seasons of life for the purpose of survival. When the music is too loud, blocking your ears is the intelligent thing to do until you're old enough to face it. God mapped out the journey so that truth comes in stages, not in seconds.

Key Bible Verse:

"I have much more to say to you, more than you can now bear" (John 16:12).

"Pick up your mat and walk" (John 5:8).
Take a P.I.C.T.U.R.E. of Temptation

P - Pain

The feeling of being tempted. The fear of being caught doing something wrong. The feeling of being trapped after you have fallen into temptation.

I - Incident

A time when I broke into a relative's closet to take his pornographic pictures. The struggle to find them in a messy closet and to do so in a swift manner without getting caught.

C - Conflict

A conflict with obstacles standing in the way of my pleasure. Underneath it all, a battle with sin.

T - Truth

Lessons about temptation—it increases with resistance, it causes you to settle for less than what you want, it ends in a snare.

U - Unfolding Action

Inciting Moment: Rummaging through the closet in search of porn. Rising Action: All of the obstacles between me and the porn. Climax: The owner arriving.

R - Resolution

The insect landing on the fly-paper. The realization that I also was trapped.

E - Empathy

Looking at the world through the eyes of a lustful pre-teen.

A Parable on Temptation

A mosquito zigzagged around the sweet-scented flypaper just above my head as I rummaged through the closet for one of those Polaroids of pleasure. With only seconds to capture what I coveted, knowing the owner would return to his bedroom any moment, I tossed aside random boxes, creased blankets, and mismatched boots in search of that hefty bag brimming with snapshots. Between the bothersome buzzing of the mosquito, the dread of the owner storming into the room, and the countless miscellaneous items I pressed through it all like a dog gnaws at the bone for whatever meat particles remain. Ironically, all the resistance I encountered in pursuit of my pleasure only intensified my cravings. The more I couldn't get to what I wanted, the more I had to have it. Resistance seems to be one of the primary ingredients in the recipe of temptation.

Finally, I found that beloved garbage bag buried within the back of the closet. Without any deliberation, I reached into it for whatever I could retrieve. If time permitted, I would have carefully selected an image that fit into my fantasies. I would have handpicked the perfect snapshot, a polaroid that raptured me somewhere far above my hectic world of a critical mother, toxic neighborhood, and a painful self-image. But the heat was on, and I had to settle for whatever I could seize.

Just as I padlocked the closet door, with some random polaroid buried within my boxers, the buzzing of the mosquito suddenly ceased. In that same moment, the owner returned to his bedroom with a suspicious look while I stood poker-faced. Above my head, I observed the bug struggling to escape from the spot he landed, an aromatic place he probably wished would satisfy his cravings. Tragically, the imbecilic insect chose the sticky side of the flypaper. And so did I.

Key Bible Verse:

"Then, after desire has conceived, it gives birth to sin; and sin, when it is full-grown, gives birth to death" (James 1:15).

"Pick up your mat and walk" (John 5:8).
Take a P.I.C.T.U.R.E. of Chastening

P - Pain

The pain of being corrected or rebuked for inappropriate behavior. The pain of knowing your behavior has affected others adversely.

I - Incident

A time from my elementary school years when I made a joke in class about the passing of a friend. Also, the teacher who corrected me and the classmate hurt by my words.

C - Conflict

A conflict with my teacher over her rebuke. Underneath it all, a conflict with my own pride and defensiveness.

T - Truth

The lesson that humor that hurts others is never cool.

U - Unfolding Action

Inciting Moment: My teacher correcting me for a crude joke. Rising Action: The realization that a classmate died and nobody thinks I'm funny. Climax: The classmate's girlfriend crying.

R - Resolution

The realization that I need new coping skills if the ones I have are hurting others.

E - Empathy

Looking at the world through the eyes of a cocky kid, a hurting classmate and a reprimanding teacher.

A Parable on Chastening

"Mr. Caparrelli, your so-called humor is not appreciated at a time like this," my fifth-grade substitute teacher—an austere middle-aged woman who dresses like an elderly, Italian widow along with her ebony-hair styled in a bun—verbally spanks me in the presence of my peers. Just a moment ago, she dropped a bomb that rattled my fellow pupils while cuing me to play the clown. The bomb: "Your classmate, Carlo, died yesterday by drowning after falling through the ice that covers Mashapaug Pond." Carlo was the voguish kid everyone adored, an athletic type dressed in trendy Reeboks who backflipped off the chain-link fence in the school yard to make all the girls go gaga. Most naturally, my classmates instantly respond with heavy panting while I remark aloud, "Does that means that Carlo's harem is single and available?" According to my teacher, my humor was rude. According to me, humor is like garlic. It's found in everything.

A desk behind me, I overhear one of the Luis' sweethearts sobbing with her head submerged in her crisscrossed arms. Out of all the girls, she seemed to be the closest you get to a "ride and die" in the fifth grade. I attempt to comfort her, but she's not too happy with my lack of sensitivity. My joke threw a pound of salt in an open, gushing wound.

Canvassing the classroom, I cannot find anyone to appreciate my jesting.

Perhaps humor that tickles the funny bone while puncturing the heart is far more cruel than cool. When your coping soothes you while scarring others, it's time to learn new coping mechanisms.

Key Bible Verse:

"A word fitly spoken is like apples of gold in settings of silver" (Prov. 25:11 ESV).

"Pick up your mat and walk" *(John 5:8).*
Take a P.I.C.T.U.R.E. of Divorce Aftermath

P - Pain

The discomfort of being in the middle of a battle between two people you love. The pain of feeling torn between two sides. To this very day, I often find myself managing this tension as I'm in the middle of many wars.

I - Incident

A time when I was about ten years old and my parents just split. It was my birthday party, and my father showed up completely outnumbered by mother's family. All of the thoughts and feelings of a kid who wants peace with his parents.

C - Conflict

A conflict with my mother's family. Underneath it all, a conflict with my fear of being ostracized by mom's family for sitting with my dad.

T - Truth

The observation that divorce leaves children feeling emotionally damaged. A principle of peace-making.

U - Unfolding Action

Inciting Moment: My father shows up at my birthday party outnumbered. Rising Action: I sit beside him despite my fears. Climax: I point out his bracelet to my mother.

R - Resolution

My mother compliments my father's bracelet. The realization that being in the middle is an advantageous position to bring two sides together.

E - Empathy

Looking at the world as a kid caught in the crossfire of two parents after divorce. A lonesome father wanting time with his son.

A Parable on Divorce Aftermath

It was my first birthday party since their bloody rift, and it was already feeling like a game of tug of war known as *Mikie in the Middle*. It was awkward seeing my father seated solo in the corner of the Ground Round Restaurant with that silly smirk on his face while watching a nearby, black and white television set.

Yesteryear, I would have sprinted to his side, spilling my guts about some girl I had a crush on in school. Yesteryear, he would have passed along some Italian-American, chauvinistic advice about what boys should do to win the affections of their *Juliet*, and I would have chuckled at his amusing anecdotes while blushing. But at this birthday party, the swiftness was sapped from my sprint. At this birthday party, I felt jerked around by two opposing sides. I felt that painful slashing within the soul when its beloved tribe splits in two.

Whether true or false, I believed wholeheartedly that sprinting to my father's table would have shown unfaithfulness to my mother, my Nonie, and all of those formidable women who raised me.

Loyalty was our family mantra, and members guilty of treason were frequently treated like treacherous infidels. It was the threat of rejection from the clan that hindered me from being chummy with Daddy.

In my young mind, I wanted to be faithful to my mother's family, but underneath it all, I was just fearful. Sometimes, faithful and fearful look alike.

Flying in the face of all my fears, I slid next to my father anyway while he replied with a playful headlock and a kiss to my forehead. I admired his new sterling silver bracelet as he removed it from his wrist for me to hold.

Looking over at the black and white television set, I observed the news-clip of President Ronald Reagan clutch Mikhail Gorbachev's hand in a gesture of friendship that ended the cold war. Reagan's diplomacy made me think that peace was always possible even amidst glaring differences.

Inspired, I called my mother over to the table and asked, 'Mom, isn't dad's new chain cool?"

For a second, it felt as if a small section of the Berlin Wall collapsed as she complimented him on his wristlet.

Being in the middle, although stressful, is the most

advantageous position to reconcile two opposing sides.

Key Bible Verse:

"Blessed are the peacemakers for they shall be called, sons of God" (Matt. 5:9).

"Pick up your mat and walk" (John 5:8).
Take a P.I.C.T.U.R.E of Hiding Crazy

P - Pain

The discomfort of feeling crazy or abnormal.

I - Incident

A moment from my adolescence when I was committed to Bradley Hospital for attempting suicide and confessing my desire to hurt other people. A moment when I tried to hide my craziness in the hospital from clinicians, but eventually blew my lid off.

C - Conflict

A conflict with my mother; she insisted I stay in the hospital when I didn't want to be there. Underneath that, a battle with my own pretentiousness and pseudo-personality.

T - Truth

The observation that what happens in private (in this case, the privacy of my own inner life) will eventually show itself in public. The observation that you can only hide your true colors so long before they surface.

U - Unfolding Action

Inciting Moment: My mother receives a call from doctor ready to discharge me. Rising Action: My mother threatens doctor. I keep hiding my craziness behind smiles. Climax: A clinician provokes my madness to manifest.

R - *Resolution*

The imagery of me throwing a chair at the clinician.

E - *Empathy*

Looking at the world through the eyes of a teenager who wants to be normal and a single mother who wants to get help for her sick son.

A Parable on Hiding Crazy

"Perhaps he's a bit maladjusted, but not unstable enough to remain an inpatient at Bradley Hospital," the stoic psychiatrist reported to my frantic mother. After a week of observation, the clinicians diagnosed me as moderately depressed but articulate, well-mannered and charismatic. Dialoguing daily with the white-coats, I quoted Shakespeare, expounded upon Churchill's reluctance to attend Yalta, and spoke some Arabic. Underneath the charade of intellectualism, I was more looney than Daffy Duck. "If you send him home and something happens, just know I'm suing your asses," my under-normal-circumstances sweet mother morphed into a lioness when advocating for her brood. "He has a switch. Just a little more time, and you will see what I'm talking about." She softened her tone. Only those closest to crazy know how cracked it truly is.

I smiled often. When the darling Mexican nurse dispensed my antidepressants every morning at 7:00 a.m, I smiled. When the schizophrenic kid across the hall intentionally defecated in his pants while playing "Hey, Jude" on his guitar, I smiled. When staff barked at me for having my lights on after curfew, I smiled. Even when they chucked me into my bedroom early for speaking out of turn, I at least smirked. At an early age, I discovered that a smile held the power to forge alliances, disarm opponents, and keep people from knowing what you feel. I learned that you can have more issues than *Time Magazine*, and a smile will tell the world something else. Just as Hamlet said about his scheming stepfather Claudius, "One may smile and smile and still be a villain."

After eleven days in Bradley Hospital, the pressure of the humdrum was wearing on me. Wakeup at 6:00 a.m., shower at 6:30 a.m., then meds at 7:00 a.m, support group at 8:00 a.m., yatayatayata. For crazy folks, monotony is far more torturous than any calamity. There I was, sitting jittery in my morning support group with a sensation that I imagine volcanoes experience just before eruption. "Michael, I'm not gonna tell you again. Raise your hand before speaking!" All it took was one condescending remark from the group facilitator when a metallic folding chair somehow transitioned from my hands into midair towards that facilitator's head. Given enough time and pressure, crazy will always blow its own cover.

Key Bible Verse:

"So then let us cast off the works of darkness and put on the armor of light" (Rom. 13:12 ESV).

"Pick up your mat and walk" (John 5:8).
Take a P.I.C.T.U.R.E. of Projection

P - Pain

The pain of feeling inferior to someone else. The pain of feeling belittled, judged, and looked down upon by someone else. A pain I deal with even in the present when conversing with people more educated or better-looking, or richer than I.

I - Incident

A moment from my high school years when I felt judged by a teacher who actually advocated for me. A moment when I judged harshly a teacher who helped me win a statewide contest for writing.

C - Conflict

A conflict with my teacher. Underneath it all, a battle with my own insecurities.

T - Truth

The observation that the faults you see in someone else are sometimes the faults you possess yourself. The Christ-like characteristic of being an advocate for people who don't even appreciate you.

U - Unfolding Action

Inciting Moment: Being kicked out of English class. Rising Action: Being invited back to the class by the teacher. Climax: Receiving news about the contest.

R - Resolution

The instant that I realize I won the contest due to help from the teacher I judged wrongly.

E - Empathy

Looking at the world through the eyes of a cocky, teenage kid and a teacher who wants to help, but whom I treat disrespectfully.

A Parable on Projection

"Take your books, your baseball cap, that mammoth chip on your shoulder and make your way out of my classroom!" she orders.

Mammoth? Oh, how I loathe the fact that she articulates with diction better than any thespian, and intellectually outclasses me with her robust vocabulary. Oh, how I despise the fact that she glares at me from a few inches of height-elevation–like Murphy Brown looking down on Danny Vito. I storm pass her desk. Oh, how I hate the fact that she locks eyes with me as if to say, "You don't scare me, punk." Most significantly, how I detest the fact that she possesses a deadly combo of intelligence, poise, and strength, all while being…a woman! In the world according to fifteen-year-old Michael, a woman in a position of authority cannot be trusted. Has not history proven that batting eyelashes and the right colored lipstick can maneuver a battleship in any direction they choose?

Ironically, she summons me to her office even after she ousted me from her classroom the week before, to discuss my most recent writing for the school newspaper. I show up at the meeting, squinty-eyed towards Murphy Brown, questioning her real intentions. During the meeting, she whips out her red pen, sheds light upon my grammatical errors and smirks like a dictator overlooking his minions. "She just wants to flaunt her intelligence, and make me feel inferior," I thought as she pontificates about the importance of not overusing commas. She actually believes she's called this meeting to polish up my paper. But I know the truth. This meeting is all about her stroking her own ego, making herself feel bigger by making me smaller.

Months later, after being transferred to another school for bad behavior, I receive a surprising letter from the Providence Journal Bulletin. I am flabbergasted to discover that I'm nominated for a state-wide, school-newspaper writing award. "Finally, Murphy Brown will see that I am no grasshopper," I ponder while being star-struck with myself. Wait! How on earth was my name even submitted for such a contest? I don't remember ever entering my story into this competition.

Alongside the letter, I find a note attached from the person who believed enough in me to enter it into the contest. The note was signed by Murphy Brown. Sometimes, what we perceive about people is not smoke and mirrors; it's just mirrors.

Key Bible Verse:

"Why do you see the speck in your brother's eye but do not notice the log in your own eye?" (Matt. 7:3 ESV).

"Pick up your mat and walk" (John 5:8).
Take a P.I.C.T.U.R.E of Consequences

P - Pain

The pain that comes from consequences. The suffering that comes with getting in trouble. The agony of being caught and punished for doing wrong.

I - Incident

A moment when I was seventeen years old, arrested for stealing a police car and breaking into a home. A moment that I was scared out of my wits when surrounded by the police on highway. I still get scared when pulled over by cops today.

C - Conflict

A conflict with the law. Underneath it all, a conflict with a rebellious nature that needs taming.

T - Truth

The characteristic of God's love and mercy that chases me down. The characteristic of a God who uses consequences to leash my wild nature.

U - Unfolding Action

Inciting Moment: Stealing a car. Rising Action: Breaking into home, cruising on highway in stolen car. Climax: Getting caught.

R - *Resolution*

The instant the K-9 approaches the window. The retrospective realization that I was on a short leash like the K-9.

E - *Empathy*

Looking at the world through the eyes of a foolish kid without any good sense or judgment.

A Parable on Consequences

It sounds like the opening line of a joke. Three Michaels coast down Rhode Island Interstate 95 in a police car: an African-American, a Puerto-Rican, and an Italian-American, all named Michael. Earlier that same day, the three hooligans poke around the Warwick Mall parking lot on the hunt for the right set of wheels. Within minutes, they spot a 1993 Toyota Camry parked in a shadowy setting. They break the steering column, jam a screwdriver into the ignition housing and sail off into the night. As they zip out of the parking lot, they find high-tech radio equipment in the front seat. "Holy *bleep!* We just robbed a police car!" the three Michaels utter in an angelic symphony (more like fallen angels than heavenly angels).

Rather than abandoning their efforts, they ransack the streets of an uppity neighborhood on the hunt for the right house. They zero on a home where the mail is backed up several days—a sign of a family away on vacation. At first glance, one of the Michaels expresses concern about the house looking familiar. "I think I know this house. I don't feel right about this," he says. But his concerns are quickly swept away by the other two Michaels, a synergy of mischief he finds too difficult to resist. Creeping through the home, the fretful Michael stumbles upon something that casts all doubt aside that they just barged into familiar territory. A family photograph, a piece of mail…something that makes it unquestionable they just broke into the home, not of a stranger, but flesh and blood. Once again, they prove to be a gang of misfortunate misfits.

On their way back home, the three Michaels feel for at least one second like successful bandits. No sooner do they stick their chests out like Goodfellas, one of the Michaels detects a police officer slowly pull up behind them. Minutes later, the other two Michaels are startled by a swarm of state troopers forming a blockade in front of them. With sirens blaring, and guns aimed at their hollow craniums, the three Michaels drop their heads in defeat.

Looking out the open window of the stolen cruiser, one of the Michaels spots a ferocious K-9 owned by the female arresting officer. The only thing restraining that dog from devouring his face was the chain, wrapped around its neck, gripped by the hands of its master. Like that K-9, they too had a short leash, wrapped around their souls, held by the hands of a Savior. Consequences would prove to be a leash that kept them from venturing off too far. Thank God for the grace of getting caught!

Key Bible Verse:

"Your rod and your staff, they comfort me" (Ps. 23:4).

"Pick up your mat and walk" (John 5:8).
Take a P.I.C.T.U.R.E of Obsessive Compulsive Disorder

P - Pain

The agony of losing your freedom. The pain of feeling constricted and confined. Losing one's sense of control. I have felt that pain when trapped in relationships, jobs, and other scenarios in which I did not want to be.

I - Incident

A moment when I was seventeen years old and felt constricted/confined in a juvenile jail. A moment when I resorted to the same behaviors that I saw in my mother as a kid: O.C.D behaviors that I despised.

C - Conflict

A conflict with a constricting environment. Underneath it all, a conflict with my own sense of control.

T - Truth

The observation that O.C.D is sometimes an attempt to regain control in your life when undergoing chaotic circumstances. The characteristic of stewardship my mother exhibited by taking care of what was within her sphere of influence.

U - Unfolding Action

Inciting Moment: Being Locked up. Rising Action: Losing all privileges of a free citizen. Climax: Resorting to O.C.D behaviors I saw in my mother.

R - Resolution

The instant I feel compassion for a mother I once ridiculed. Finally, understanding what drove her O.C.D behaviors.

E - Empathy

Looking at the world through the eyes of a young, single mother who tried her best to maintain orderliness and sanity amidst chaos.

A Parable on Obsessive Compulsive Disorder (O.C.D.)

For most of my childhood, I resented my mother's fanaticism. Staring at all of the canned goods lined-up with labels facing forward in an almost divine symmetry, I had this craving to make a mess out of her orderliness. Noticing the way she methodically positioned the toys on my bedroom bureau like they were imported knickknacks from France, I wanted to place the high powered fan right in front of her neat arrangement. Wearing the Fruit Of The Looms she ironed like it was a Georgio Armani suit, I had the thought of intentionally soiling my undies to send her a message. For many years, I criticized her behaviors as freakish until the day arrived when I discovered what it was all about. Never ridicule the surface of something until you see what lies beneath.

Briefly incarcerated at seventeen years old, all of my freedom was stripped from me like a caged cat. I had no more say-so over my schedule—the guards told me whether it was time for breakfast, basketball or bible study. I had no more consent over my meal choices—the kitchen staff imposed upon me the processed green-beans that gave me agita (Italian slang for acid reflux).

In the absence of freedom, what did I do? I folded the sheets on my mattress neatly like they were made of Siam silk. I lined up my books in alphabetical order like I was a librarian on the clock. I placed my sneakers in the same spot everyday like it was their home. I lived up to the words of poet Ralph Waldo Emerson "Men are what their mothers have made of them."

Reflecting upon that sixteen-year-old girl who birthed a baby boy named Mikie, I see a young woman struggling to hold onto whatever marbles were left.

The rent is due, the baby is hungry, the lenders are calling, and the husband is gone. In such a chaotic environment, what does she do? She lines up canned goods, irons underwear, and polishes her home like it's a Smithsonian museum.

Could it be that behind every case of O.C.D, there is a God-given need to bring chaos back into order? Mom, you not only held onto your marbles, but you kept them shiny.

Key Bible Verse:

"Whatever you do, work heartily, as for the Lord and not for men" (Col. 3:23 ESV).

"Pick up your mat and walk" (John 5:8).
Take a P.I.C.T.U.R.E. of Egotism

P - *Pain*

The pain of egotism's results. The embarrassment that comes from being exposed as not as great as you are supposed to be.

I - *Incident*

A time when I took my girlfriend to New York City to show off my knowledge of the city and ended up humiliated after being hustled in a card game.

C - *Conflict*

A conflict with a conman. Underneath it all, a battle with my own ego.

T - *Truth*

Lessons about egotism—pride comes before a fall.

U - *Unfolding Action*

Inciting Moment: The decision to flaunt my knowledge of the city to girlfriend. Rising Action: Putting up money on a card game. Climax: Finding out that all three cards were bent as the Middle eastern guy vanished.

R - *Resolution*

Losing my money, and realizing that my own pride made a fool of me.

E - Empathy

Looking at the world through the eyes of a big-headed young man.

A Parable on Egotism

Egotism comes with the turf of being eighteen years old. That's how I like to preface this story to spare myself the total disgrace of being taken in by a New York City card-shark. From the days of my youth, I visited the city religiously with my Bronx-native stepfather Freddy, a proud Yankee who squinted his eyes and cocked his head back like DeNiro while speaking in the tongue of Tremont Avenue (same setting as the film, *Bronx Tale*). Following Freddy's lead, I learned where to find the sweetest cannoli, the most sizzling pizza, the best bargains, and a host of other insider-tips on all five boroughs. Now, on July 4, 1997, it was the moment to flaunt my urban acumen to a new girlfriend, a cute blonde with the high cheekbones of a southern belle, who never bit before into the Big Apple. Regrettably so, my cockiness always paved the way for blunders that made a buffoon out of me: playing the big shot always resulted in playing the fool.

"What's that black dude doing across the street, shuffling the cards?" my southern belle inquired with the innocence of a puppy lost in the Amazon. "He's hustling people for their money. But I got what it takes to take what he got," I replied. "Here's how he works it, baby. He lets you win the first hand, so that you will raise your biddings the second hand, and then he crushes you. But here's how we work it. We play the first hand, then beat it with our profits before he beats us."

The second we stepped into the flimflam, it was all over before it started. "Follow the queen, follow the queen," he spit the words out like an auctioneer at high bidding. As I predicted,

I won the first hand, converting my Ulysses Grant greenback into a Ben Franklin. But just as we were about to skedaddle, a towering Middle Eastern man taps me on the shoulder whispering, "Seems like the deck is unmanned." I noticed the young kid abandoned the cards on his table to chit-chat with a friend. "How about we go in together on a deal? I'll slightly bend the queen, making it detectable to win," the Middle Eastern man offered. Bet! What a great opportunity to not only quadruple my winnings but show my girlfriend the stuff that makes me. When the kid returned to the table, he shuffled the cards so fast I couldn't even see him bending all three. After he beat me for every penny in my pocket, I scanned the crowd for the Middle-Eastern man. He pulled a Houdini before the game was even over. Pride always makes an easy mark out of a man.

Key Bible Verse:

"Pride goes before destruction, and a haughty spirit before a fall" (Prov. 16:1).

"Pick up your mat and walk" (John 5:8).
Take a P.I.C.T.U.R.E. of Injustice

P - Pain

The discomfort of being a witness to injustice. To this very day, anytime I see injustice, I feel angst until I do something to make the crooked path straight.

I - Incident

A time when I was a young adult busboy at a restaurant working for a waiter who refused to seat African-Americans. I sat them in our section anyway despite his instruction not to seat them.

C - Conflict

A conflict with my waiter. Underneath it all, a conflict with my own people-pleasing tendencies.

T - Truth

The principle that it pleases God to help the vulnerable rather than please the powerful.

U - Unfolding Action

Inciting Moment: An African-American family waiting a long time for a table. Rising Action: My manager refusing to seat them. Climax: I seat them anyway.

R - Resolution

The little girl smiling at me as I hand her the Barbie doll while a priest walks by and winks. The realization that God is pleased when I reach out to the rejected.

E - Empathy

Looking at the world through the eyes of a rejected people and a people-pleasing young man wanting to do what is right.

A Parable on Injustice

It was a buzzing Saturday night at Rhode Island's most sentimental restaurant, and throngs of folks twiddled their thumbs for a minimum of one hour in its congested foyer. Guys told stories of the good ol' days, wives tamed their naughty children while one particular family patiently waited longer than everyone else. I mean, they could have completed *The Godfather* trilogy, and still been kicking their heels when the flicks were over. The husband had a newscaster face dressed in a debonair suit, arm in arm with a wife who looked like she leaped off the cover of *Ebony* magazine. Their children conducted themselves like characters from a 1950s sitcom, standing out in a foyer filled with bratty kids, even requesting permission to make a bathroom trip. An hour wait became more than two, but they survived the wait with class. I told my waiter Billy, "I'm gonna seat that family at table seven." He replied, "Don't you dare! Colored don't tip well."

Being an amateur busboy with the job that everyone in the neighborhood coveted, the pressure to please was on. Whatever my waiter asked of me, short of wiping his backside, I did. The ornery lady with whiskers wants more butter on her buns. *I got it!* The fella boasting about his stocks to impress his girlfriend wants ketchup. *I got it!* The patronizing city councilman who doodles his schemes on napkins demands a takeout container. *I got it!* Under such intensity to please the powers that be, I looked over at the outcast family with an urge to make things a little easier for them. Sometimes, we who aim to please stand betwixt two parties beckoning us from different sides of the aisle, and a decision must be made.

As Billy entered the dining room, he nearly spit his coffee out when he caught a glimpse of the "colored" folks comfortably seated at table seven. "This is coming out of your *scarole*," he whispered, using Italian slang for money in his wanna-be mafioso tone.

How I wished to God they tipped generously just to preserve my status! It ended up being a tad over seventeen percent. Of course, Billy played it up like it was the worse tip in the world, forgetting the countless Caucasians who left pocket change.

A minute later, their little girl returned for her Barbie doll. As I handed her the doll, she smiled. Strangely enough, a Catholic priest walking by at the same time winked at me. If faced with the choice of pleasing the lofty or the lowly, choose the lowly.

The former earns you a pat on the back from people; the

latter gets you a wink from the Man Upstairs.

Key Bible Verse:

"For though the Lord is high, He regards the lowly" (Ps. 138:6 ESV).

"Pick up your mat and walk" (John 5:8).
Take a P.I.C.T.U.R.E. of Ridicule

P - *Pain*

The pain of biting your tongue when ridiculed.

I - *Incident*

A time when I was a young adult car salesman and publicly berated by my sales manager. A moment when I wanted to react but was encouraged by a fellow associate to not react.

C - *Conflict*

A conflict with my sales manager. Underneath it all, a conflict with my own retaliating nature.

T - *Truth*

The principle that to ignore a person's ridicule is sometimes more effective than to offer a reply.

U - *Unfolding Action*

Inciting Moment: My manager ridicules me. Rising Action: My struggle to not react. Climax: I follow my associate's encouragement to not respond.

R - *Resolution*

My sales manager apologized to me the next day. My realization that to ignore him was more effective way to shed light on his bad behavior.

E - Empathy

Look at the world through the eyes of a short-tempered young man who bites his tongue.

A Parable on Ridicule

As he spews the kind of vulgarity in my face that would make Howard Stern blush, he grossly underestimates how much animal still lives within me. For a moment, I see what he sees when he glares at me—a twenty-three-year-old, clean-cut, Bible college student hustling used cars on the side to support his newlywed wife and infant son. But what he doesn't discern is that underneath the clergy collar, violent impulses buzz within me like buttons blaring on a control panel during some sort of crisis. In a frenzied moment like this, I can't help but think, "Puncture his ear-drum with that number two pencil sitting on his keyboard. Drive the nearby 2003 Honda Pilot into the sales desk. Wrap the lamp cord around his neck until you hear a medic holler, "*Code Blue!*" Not just scoundrels, but saints too seek for reprisal. If you scream long enough in someone's face, even a nun is capable of hitting you with a tire iron.

Had it not been for Sean whispering in my ear a second ago, I would have fired back. Being an old hand in the car business, as well as a veteran of life long enough to experience the tradeoff of egotism for wisdom, Sean knows just what to say to me. He has been around this block many times before with sales managers. Just before I shoot back, Sean whispers in my ear, "You need not say anything. He will self-destruct." Looking over at the sales manager, I see him unraveling as I bite my tongue. Noticing the vein in his neck bulge, I remember a statement from Pastor Manzo's sermon few months earlier that corroborated

Sean's counsel. "You need not retaliate because every Judas hangs himself." In a moment that could have turned into a *Dateline* episode, I defuse the situation by using my ignore muscle.

A few days later, the sales manager catches me alone during my lunch break while seated at a picnic table overlooking our used car inventory. Anticipating a fight, I clench my jaw. Instead, he speaks softly with an air of innocence. "Mike, I'm sorry for the horrible things I said to you during that deal last weekend. He extends a hand which I shake. Watching the repentant sales manager mosey away, I am reminded of the sheer brilliance of using your ignore muscle. Had I fought fire with fire, the only thing that the sales manager would have pondered over the last few days would have been my bad behavior. By using my ignore muscle, I gave him no reaction, therefore there was no distractions from reflecting upon his own shameful misdeeds.

Key Bible Verse:

"But (Jesus) gave him no answer, not even to a single charge" (Matt. 27:14 ESV).

"Pick up your mat and walk" (John 5:8).
Take a P.I.C.T.U.R.E. of Favor

P - Pain

The pressure that comes from being favored. The pressure of having to please the one who favors you so you don't lose that favor. The turmoil that comes from being hated by jealous people.

I - Incident

An incident when I was favored by my boss who offered me

a part-time position in a company that wasn't allowed to anyone else. The jealousy from others over that favor. The owner's method of making it fair for everyone.

C - Conflict

A conflict with my colleagues. Underneath it all, a conflict with the fear of man.

T - Truth

The observation that favor brings haters, and that the favor of God is more important than the favor of men.

U - Unfolding Action

Inciting Moment: The owner showing me unusual favor. Rising Action: The ensuing jealousy of colleagues. Climax: Telling the owner that I couldn't accept the favor, and his decision to make part-time positions available for everyone.

R - Resolution

The decision I made to not receive the favor lest I should lose the favor of God.

E - Empathy

Looking at the world through the eyes of a people-pleasing young man, and a gracious owner of a company.

A Parable on Favor

I knew I found favor with the Big Dog the instant he summoned me into his office, chucked a duffel bag of $50,000 towards my feet, and asked me to deposit the Scarola (Italian slang for money) into his account. "Straight to the bank kid, ya hear?" he stated with his Italian-American, staccato dialect. I was unsure why he would confide in a twenty-two-year-old whippersnapper salesman with a juvenile history of shenanigans.

I was also unclear as to why he snubbed so many of my fellow sales-people while religiously inviting me to breakfast at the Lighthouse Restaurant. Sometimes, favor descends upon you without any rhyme or reason, an influence over someone that's so odd, it can only be God.

Perhaps the finest example of this favor was when the Big Dog offered me part-time hours, allowing me to work prime-time every evening, while not requiring me to be present during the hum-drum mornings. He dangled that carrot before me when he discovered I was leaving his empire to pursue a theology degree at a local Bible college.

A short time after his offer, the news spread amongst my peers that I was being crowned with such courtesy, stirring up animosity towards me. "What's with this bull*bleep!* Caparrelli strolls in at five o'clock with his Bible and stupid smirk while we twiddle our thumbs all day!"

Little is the likelihood of gaining favor and keeping your friends all at the same time.

One morning, I tiptoed into the Big Dog's office to tell him what I knew he didn't want to hear. "Mike, I'm sorry but I can't accept your offer. I fear the day will come when you and I will lose our friendship because of the stress added to your life for letting me work part time. Your employees aren't too happy with the decision. It's not fair to them," I said sheepishly. "What do you mean, it's not fair? I'll make it fair right now."

He snatched the nearby intercom receiver from the wall, hollered into it as if he were talking into a freakin' tin-can. "A new rule at Metro Honda that applies to everyone, so listen up! If any sales person wants to attend Bible college, they don't have to work morning hours!"

Albeit an endearing gesture, I still didn't accept his offer, a decision that I believe preserved our friendship for the next eighteen years. Sometimes, you have to say "no" to certain favors in order to hold onto a greater favor.

Key Bible Verse:

"I will accept nothing belonging to you. You will never be able to say, 'I made Abram rich'" (Gen. 14:23).

"Pick up your mat and walk" (John 5:8).
Take a P.I.C.T.U.R.E. of Love

P - *Pain*

The pain that comes with love. The struggle of winning the affections of someone who rejects you. The willingness to persevere towards love even when shunned.

I - *Incident*

A time when I was a young parent, trying to win the affections of my then stepdaughter (now, my daughter). All of the measures I took to win her affection, and all the ways she rejected me in return.

C - *Conflict*

A conflict with Ashley. Underneath it all, a conflict with my own fear of rejection and love-exhaustion.

T - *Truth*

The observation that love never fails. The principle that the best kind of love is letting them go so that they return on their own terms.

U - *Unfolding Action*

Inciting Moment: Church lady telling me I should drop the "step" in "stepdaughter." Rising Action: All of my attempts to win her love. Climax: Letting her go.

R - *Resolution*

The text-message in which she called me *Dad*. The realization that I had to let her go for her to come to me on her own.

E - *Empathy*

Looking at the world through the eyes of a father eager to win his daughter's love, and a daughter needing to find her own way.

A Parable on Love

"Pastor Mike, may I say something to you? I hope you don't take offense in what I'm about to say, but I think you should call Ashley your daughter rather than your stepdaughter," the church lady said. Truth be told, every ounce of oxytocin I possessed yearned to claim that golden beauty as my own. From the day I married her mother, I fell in love with her mischievous smile, Goldilocks hair and avant-garde style. From the moment I said "I do" to her mother, I said "I will" to myself about winning her heart. But, my intuition told me having her love necessitated a fight.

My first punch was an uppercut with *money*. As we pulled our car into Ashley's driveway to pick her up for weekly visitations from her dad, her mother and I resolved to pay full child support on my income as a car salesman even though it wasn't stipulated by the courts. But, with each pickup, sassy Ashley sunk her petite frame into the backseat with very little to say other than tormenting me with a few words about her latest boyfriend named Pierre. Whatever money we doled out never made any difference in our relationship.

My first K.O. (Knock Out) was realizing that Ashley's love couldn't be bought but had to be sought. My second punch was a right hook with *time*.

Shortly after we resumed full-custody of Ashley, when she was eleven, I made it a discipline to wake up early to watch her beloved pastime, *Buffy the Vampire Slayer*, before she bolted to school. And boy, did I catch a verbal whipping from a couple of religious folks about that decision! How could an associate pastor watch such ghoulish programming with his offspring? I didn't give a rat's rear-end what they said; it was a chance to be with her. But, most mornings, there wasn't much dialogue between us. Instead, Ashley sat quietly under Buffy's trance as I sat quietly. My second K.O. was realizing that connecting with her was so much more than merely convening with her.

Over the years, there were many more punches thrown. I never liked it when people asked, "Are you a fighter or a lover?" How can one be a lover without being a fighter? Years later, after she left home, she texted me one day, "Dad, what are you doing?" I spit my spaghetti out of my mouth. "She called me *Dad!*" From then on, our bond was thicker than blood. My last K.O. was realizing that what makes something your own is when it comes to you, all on its own.

Key Bible Verse: "Love bears all things, believes all things, hopes all things, endures all things" (1 Cor. 13:7 ESV).

"Pick up your mat and walk" (John 5:8).
Take a P.I.C.T.U.R.E. of Anxiety

P - Pain

The anxiety that comes from being late, not performing up to par, and not pleasing the people I respect. The anxiety of not having what it takes to get the job done.

I - Incident

My first day on the job as a full-time minister in a church. I'm running late for work, and I accidentally place my coffee mug on top of the car before I drive off. I find the coffee mug still in place when I arrive.

C - Conflict

A conflict with time running out. Underneath it all, a conflict with my own anxieties over not measuring up.

T - Truth

The observation that anxiety breeds more anxiety, and lots of mistakes along the way. The observation that peace gives you poise in the midst of turbulence.

U - Unfolding Action

Inciting Moment: Noticing that I'm running late for work. Rising Action: The anxious thoughts on the way to work. Climax: The sight of my coffee mug still situated on top of the car.

R - Resolution

The realization that the mug is a metaphor teaching me that God wants to give me peace that gives me poise even in the midst of turbulence.

E - Empathy

Looking at the world through an anxious young man on his first day at work.

A Parable on Anxiety

I smooch the wife goodbye, drape my Gap-styled jean bag over my shoulders, snatch my most sentimental coffee mug (a beaker that features an embroidered picture of my family) and dash out the door like the house is on fire. It is March 1, 2004, my first day on the job of full time ministry serving under Pastor Manzo, a stickler of time-management. Glancing at my watch, I have nine minutes to execute a fifteen-minute commute to work! Just about to pull out of my countryside driveway, I have that dreadful feeling of forgetting something. Being in such a frenzy, my thoughts are too rapid to remember what I'm forgetting so I bolt out the driveway. Anxiety makes you an exceedingly fast mover but an exceptionally-flawed thinker.

Rocketing towards the church in a Barney-purple Nissan Altima, I fretfully anticipate storming into the office several minutes tardy as the new Ministries Director. I imagine what Pastor Manzo will think of me: *"If this kid cannot handle showing up to work on time, how will he manage being present at the wake of some emergency?"* As I cut an elderly lady off, I reflect upon all of the challenges associated with full-time ministry in a recovery-based church. The thought of drug overdoses and domestic disturbances raises my cortisol levels. I work myself into a frenzy while assessing my own incompetence in the face of such heavy demands. I can't even get to work on time, never mind flying with a cape over the city! The more I fret, the more I sweat. Anxiety, itself, becomes the mother of all anxiety.

Tranquility oozes out of my body as I notice Pastor Manzo standing behind the glass office door while I pull into the church parking lot. Instinctively, I pray for the peace of God as I swiftly exit my car.

"What am I forgetting?" I ask myself one more time as I shut the driver door behind me. "My coffee!" The thought flashes like a shooting star. Looking up, I notice that I left my sentimental coffee mug on the top of the vehicle.

Thinking nothing of it, I snatch the mug and head towards the office door. *Wait! How on earth did that mug remain still, fixed in one position on top of the vehicle, for a ten-mile commute? How did the mug maintain its composure amidst wind, motion and velocity?* Immediately, the Holy Spirit enlightens me to the kind of peace that God will grant me for the next sixteen years of ministry. Like the mug, peace maintains its composure, remains perfectly still, even in the midst of turbulence.

Key Bible Verse:

"And the peace of God which surpasses all understanding will guard your hearts and minds in Christ Jesus" (Phil. 4:7).

"Pick up your mat and walk" (John 5:8).
Take a P.I.C.T.U.R.E. of Stigma

P - Pain

The distress of feeling accused of something you didn't do, based on your past actions. The pain of feeling stigmatized because of your previous wrongdoings. Most of these feelings are strictly imaginary but very real in my emotions.

I - Incident

A time when my church was robbed and I felt like I was being accused of the robbery based on my history. The culprit turns himself in, and my pastor trusts me with the money to retrieve the computer.

C - Conflict

A conflict with a church lady whom I mistakenly perceive as accusing me of a crime I didn't commit. Underneath it all, a conflict with my own self-image and heightened sensitivity to how others perceive me.

T - Truth

The characteristic of a church that loved and accepted me, not despite my past, but because of my past.

U - Unfolding Action

Inciting Moment: The church robbery. Rising Action: Being questioned about my whereabouts the night it was robbed. Climax: The culprit turning himself in, my pastor trusting me.

R - Resolution

My pastor telling me that my past experiences is the reason why he trusts me to carry out this deed.

E - Empathy

Looking at the world through a young man, who feels stigmatized because of his past actions, and a gracious man of God, who sees the best in people.

A Parable on Stigma

"Who would be heartless enough to rob the house of God?" I overhear a voice murmur while we quasi-detectives investigate the crime scene. My office window wide-open, a disheveled desk and my colleague's missing laptop; it's clear someone among us still has sticky fingers. The suspects are endless in a congregation thronged with misfits. Former drug addicts, bank robbers, knee-breakers, and me make up the bunch. Ironically, I made an attempt to knock off this same church, even breaking a window, ten years prior to being appointed on the pastoral staff. Apparently, this is the church where you are loved and accepted *despite* your past.

For a minute, it feels like the spotlight of suspicion zeroes in on me. "Where were you last night, Mike?" she interrogates in what I perceive as a dubious tone. "Home with the kids. Why do you ask?" I reply while my blood-pressure skyrockets like it did when I was busted at seventeen for robbing a police car. "Just thought you may have attended the prayer meeting last night, and seen something?" she responds. Feeling like a suspect, I sweat profusely knowing that yesteryear's misdeeds are forgiven but not forgotten. But it's all in my head. I have to remind myself, "This is the church where you are loved and accepted *despite* your past."

Fortunately, the culprit among us turns himself in. To nobody's surprise, it was an addict seeking for the means to get a quick fix. My pastor, a former criminal-mastermind himself, insists on retrieving the laptop in light of its confidential data. He turns to me, handing over an envelope of cash along with a note, and says, "Our culprit says we can recover the laptop from this guy's house. He's a drug-dealer in the Olneyville area and wants two-fifty cash for the computer. His address is on this note." Flabbergasted by his level of trust in me, I ask, "Why do you want me to go?" Without hesitation, he responds, "Because you're the only one on this staff who knows these streets." Suddenly, it dawns on me that this is not the church where you are chosen *despite* your past; this is the church where you are chosen *because* of your past.

Key Bible Verse:

"God chose the lowly things of this world and the despised things" (1 Cor. 1:28).

"Pick up your mat and walk" *(John 5:8).*

Take a P.I.C.T.U.R.E. of Awkward Bonding

P - *Pain*

The awkwardness of intimacy. The uncomfortable feelings that ensue from bonding with another male. The barrier of pride and intolerant thinking that stands in the way of bonding with people older than I.

I - *Incident*

A moment from my young adulthood when my father made an attempt to spend quality time with me over some hot dogs. A moment when I struggled with meeting him half-way.

C - *Conflict*

A conflict with my father's inability to show affection. Underneath it all, a conflict with my own stubbornness and intolerance towards my dad's weaknesses.

T - *Truth*

The principle of honoring your elders by showing compassion for their limitations, and following their lead rather than insisting they follow yours.

U - *Unfolding Action*

Inciting Moment: My dad inviting me for lunch. Rising Action: My father getting upset because I'm ignoring him. Climax: Turning away from my work to address my father plainly.

R - *Resolution*

The imagery of me shutting down my computer to accompany my father.

E - *Empathy*

Looking at the world through the eyes of a grown man, despite his limitations, trying to bond with his son.

A Parable on Awkward Bonding

"I'm headed to the joint across the street for a hot dog," he mumbles while dilly-dallying near my office door with his left hand on the knob while signaling my attention with the other. Garbed in a black-leather motorcycle jacket with his hair greased back like 1970's Travolta, he looks like your quintessential, Italo-American tough-guy father. But there is a peculiar sound I hear in his voice that does not jive with his bad-boy persona. I detect he's feeling mushy on this autumn afternoon. Perhaps he just watched a Hallmark movie. I discern that his statement about the "hot dog joint" is more of an invitation than just information. He is asking me to join him for some father-son quality time. When you receive an invitation to bond with an old-schooler, it's not usually written in straight-forward language; instead, it requires some translating.

"I'm headed to the joint across the street for a hot dog," he says a second time while slightly perturbed that I'm not catching on to his invite. My face remains buried in my laptop while faking oblivion. "Good for you, Dad! Enjoy the hot dog!" I reply without even looking his way. I know what he means behind what he says, but I refuse to acknowledge the invitation until it's been clearly issued. "If you want me to join you for a hot dog, then ask the question, Pops," I say to myself. Facts are, my father exhibits his love through provision, but struggles with showing it through words of affection. The generational gap widens as the younger demand for elders to speak their language rather than learning to understand the language of their elders.

"I'm heading to the joint across the street for a hot dog!" he utters a third time, only much louder, undeniably annoyed by my lack of feedback. Out of nowhere, I sense compassion spring up towards him. For the first time, I feel for his struggle in asking me a question he did not have the will or words to articulate. "Dad, do you want me to join you for some wieners?" Swallowing my massive ego, I verbalize the question for him. "I don't give a damn what you do," he replies, irritated, shrugging his shoulders while rolling his eyes. Smirking at his comical response, I rise from my desk and shut my laptop screen.

Out the door, father and son head to the joint across the street for some wieners and fries. If there shall be any bonding between older and younger, someone has to hear what's being said. Who goes first? He with ears, let him hear.

Key Bible Verse:

"Honor your father and mother so that you may live long in the land the Lord God is giving you" (Ex. 20:12).

"Pick up your mat and walk" (John 5:8).
Take a P.I.C.T.U.R.E of Loneliness

P - Pain

The pain of loneliness, feeling forsaken, alone in struggles. The pain of nobody understanding me.

I - Incident

A moment when I was forty years old and had a heart attack. I woke up from a nightmare in which I was surrounded by people in a ballroom and couldn't communicate with them. Felt alienated from everyone. Woke up to my little girl snuggling with me.

C - Conflict

A conflict with people who don't understand me. Underneath that, a battle with my own feelings of being forsaken.

T - Truth

The observation that loneliness is not a physical reality but emotional reality. Loneliness is the absence of being understood by people. Also, some light on the characteristic of empathy, the ability to respond to the unspoken cries of others.

U - Unfolding Action

Inciting Moment: Reference to the heart attack. Rising Action: Not being understood by others, the nightmare, etc. Climax: During the nightmare, the inability to utter a word as I try to scream for help.

R - Resolution

The instant I realize my daughter wrapped her arms around me.

E - Empathy

Looking at the world through the eyes of a lonely guy during his darkest hour, and an empathetic daughter.

A Parable on Loneliness

At forty, I felt altogether lonesome after being dumbfounded by a heart attack. Don't get me wrong, dozens of get-well cards stockpiled on the kitchen counter, hundreds of folks reached out through social media in addition to all the gregarious, Italian-American relatives who visited our home. Yet, amidst the masses, I felt like a foreigner in a land where I couldn't speak the language. "How are you doing, Pastor Mike?" folks sincerely enquired. Unlike me, it seemed impossible to articulate my utter abandonment. I understood Tom Hanks in *Castaway*, when the most he could do was grunt after being deserted for several years. Hence, the gap between others and I grew, at least in my dark mind. The apex of loneliness is when there's hundreds of people *near* you, yet you cannot find one single soul to *hear* you.

In the dead of night, I dreamt of making an effort to scream in a ballroom congested with people, yet not a mere vibration emitted from my mouth. Veins bulged from my neck and my eyeballs protruded from their sockets as I strained to holler for help. Yet, nothing was heard by the masses. Outside the dream, I felt warmth surge through my soul as an arm wrapped around my comatose body. In that lonely moment, my twelve-year-old daughter Olivia snuggled close to her beloved dad. Empathy is a knack to respond to the unspoken cry of another person.

That evening, there wasn't much said between my daughter and me. All of her life, she was a matter-of-fact kid who did not readily express her affections. She could easily argue her opinion on matters like a skillful attorney while at the same time withholding her deepest feelings. In our home, Olivia was a kid whose head rules her heart. Yet, in this moment, her arm does all of the talking. Sometimes, the most meaningful communication cannot be heard with ears but is felt with the heart—nonverbal statements that let you know unequivocally, "You have not been forsaken."

Key Bible Verse:

"Also, if two lie down together, they will keep warm. But how can one keep warm alone?" (Eccles. 4:11).

"Pick up your mat and walk" (John 5:8).
Take a P.I.C.T.U.R.E of Being Wrongly Judged

P - Pain

The feeling of being wrongly perceived by others. The annoyance that comes from being judged mistakenly while doing a good deed. Even to this day, I dislike it when people stare at me through cynical eyes.

I - Incident

A moment when I first planted a church in Rhode Island, and saw a prostitute in the neighborhood. A moment when I reached out to her and felt judged by the people of the neighborhood. The interactions between the prostitute and myself that opened my eyes.

C - Conflict

A conflict with public opinion. Underneath it all, a conflict with my own desire to look good before others rather than looking good before God.

T - Truth

The characteristic of Jesus in being a friend of sinners, regardless of what people thought about him.

U - Unfolding Action

Inciting Moment: Picking up a prostitute. Rising Action: Dialogue with the prostitute. Learning about her own story. Climax: Sharing Jesus with her.

R - Resolution

The instant I hear about her going to prison, becoming a Christian, and entering a Teen Challenge drug rehab.

E - Empathy

Looking at the world through the eyes of a working girl who carries maternal guilt with her.

A Parable on Being Wrongly Judged

It is your typical Monday morning in suburbia. Sappy mothers smooch their kids on the cheek, crossing guards escort little ones towards the school bus, retirees gas up their lawnmowers and…a tipsy hooker meanders through the neighborhood. Huh? The second I spot her shapely figure against the backdrop of this Normal Rockwell scenery, I hear that song from *Sesame Street* play, "One of these things is not like the others." The working girl provocatively waves at the traffic, moms respond with sanctimony and the retirees drop their jaws. I could read the minds of these white-bread suburbanites: "Get her the hell out of the neighborhood!"

"How much for twenty minutes?" Without carefully thinking it through, I holler at her through my side window as I pull up just a few feet away. Looking into the rear-view mirror, I notice a crossing-guard gawking at me. I question whether she knows who I am. I wonder if she saw me on the public access channel for our weekly broadcast. "Thirty dollars," the working girl responds with a pretty Irish smile symmetrically positioned a few inches below her calloused eyes. Flying in the face of my reservations, I signal her to enter. As she steps into the passenger seat, I foresee the newspaper headline flashing before me: *Local Pastor Picks Up a Hooker.*

On the quest for an obscure spot to complete our transaction, she asks me to stop in front of a cape-style home. In the backyard, I notice one of those K-mart playgrounds that are just as cool to a five-year-old as an amusement park. "My daughter lives here with my mother. It's been a while since I seen her face," she says with deep maternal pain. We speed off with a trail of tears behind us. A few minutes later, we pull into a random parking lot. "Here's your thirty dollars, but I'm not looking for sex. I just want you to know that Jesus loves you." She's just as surprised by me as I am by her. Behind the facade of what seems a perverted customer is a caring pastor. Underneath the charade of what appears a calloused hooker is a hurting mother.

A few months later, a woman spooks me in our church foyer with an embarrassing question. "Pastor Mike, did you pick up a hooker a few months back?" she asks loudly while I blush. "Excuse me?" I whisper. "That girl you picked up accepted Jesus. She's now a student at Teen Challenge drug rehab and doing wonderful. She asked me to thank you for reaching out." Right there, I'm reminded of the Savior who'd rather do good than look good.

Key Bible Verse:

Jesus was "a friend of tax collectors and sinners" (Matt. 11:19).

"Pick up your mat and walk" (John 5:8).
Take a P.I.C.T.U.R.E of Incompetence

P - *Pain*

The pain of feeling inadequate or incompetent for a task. The uneasiness that comes with biting off more than you can chew. My entire life, I have committed myself to projects too big for me, and have suffered in various ways from that behavior.

I - *Incident*

115

A time when I took a large group of people to New York City for an outing, most of whom had no knowledge of the city. A situation whereby we were running late for the subway and only half the group made it on the train.

C - Conflict

A conflict with time running out. Underneath it all, a conflict with my own feelings of inadequacy in the area of leadership.

T - Truth

Lessons about leadership: Confusion rolls downhill, listening to the voices of people more than your own gut will cost you and leadership without followers is not leadership at all.

U - Unfolding Action

Inciting Moment: Confusion over directions to the subway. Rising Action: Time running out while I take wrong turns and emotionally unravel. Climax: Barely making it on the subway train.

R - Resolution

The instant I realized that half my group missed the train.

E - Empathy

Looking at the world through the eyes of confused followers and an inexperienced leader.

A Parable on Incompetence

It was our first church expedition in July 2010, and I bit off more elephant than I could chew. What would ever possess me to facilitate an outing of thirty-five suburbanites to sensory–overloaded New York City is a subject the cherubs still chuckle over in heaven. "That boy's crazy," remarked the archangel Gabrielle. The entire day was planned meticulously, from a sentimental afternoon in Ellis Island to a spirit-filled evening at

Brooklyn Tabernacle, all except one detail: the subway commute. I figured I rely upon twenty years of NYC experiences to navigate, but underestimated the need of my followers for crystal-clear directions. While I could handle the "trial and error" stroll from the parking garage to the subway, church folks stressed under the *"Take a left. My apologies, take a right"* supervision of Pastor Mike. Joe Tufano, one of my favorite grumpy old men, looked like he wanted to puncture me in the throat with a number two pencil.

Leadership Observation Number One: A slight mist of confusion to the captain equates to a heavy fog of chaos over his team. If the leader scratches his head, the constituents pull out their hair.

Confusion often paves the way for a cacophony of opinions. "I think we'd be better off parking near the ferry so we don't have to take the subway," one ruddy-faced brother interjected. "I say we abandon the Ellis Island idea and get a pizza," a sweat-drenched sister chimed in. Standing still in an Upper-Westside neighborhood, unsure of my next move, I fought hard to maintain a semblance of focus.

Leadership Observation Number Two: The breakdown of leadership begins when the voices in the crowd becomes louder than the still voice within.

When we finally arrived at the subway station, we had less than two minutes to board the train. Marching towards Terminal B like General MacArthur invading Normandy, I led the way. Unlike MacArthur who had all of his troops marching closely behind him, almost half my team sauntered quite a distance behind me.

"Pastor Mike, aren't we going to wait for the rest of the group?" someone asked. "You snooze, you lose," I arrogantly responded. In the nick of time, I stepped onto the train along with the door gliding behind me.

Staring through the closed subway door window, it was painfully clear that a handful of the suburbanites never made it on the train. It was like a scene from an end-times movie—one will be taken up in the air while the other is left behind.

Leadership Observation Number Three: A leader who loses followers is a man taking a walk.

Key Bible Verse:

"The Lord will make you the head, not the tail" (Deut. 28:13).

"Pick up your mat and walk" (John 5:8).
Take a P.I.C.T.U.R.E of Pressure

P - Pain

The frustration of not being able to provide something. The pressure to come up with resources you do not have. The pain of letting someone you love down/disappointing someone. It's a pain that haunts me in my present day relationships and causes me to work hard.

I - Incident

A time when I took my family to Six Flags with very little money. My little girl wanted ice cream after seeing a family eating some. I looked for some way of getting her what she wanted.

C - Conflict

A conflict with a lack of resources. Underneath it all, a battle with my self-concept as a father.

T - Truth

The observation that opportunity presents itself in unusual ways. The principle of seizing the opportunities that come disguised as difficulties.

U - Unfolding Action

Inciting Moment: My daughter asking for ice cream. Rising Action: The ride not working accompanied by my daughter's disappointment. Climax: My conversation with the manager.

R - Resolution

The manager giving us vouchers for free ice cream. The realization about opportunities coming in disguise.

E - Empathy

Looking at the world through the eyes of a hungry little girl, and a father eager to please his daughter.

A Parable on Pressure

"Daddy, let's get ice cream." My five-year old daughter Olivia petitioned me in that even-textured voice she inherited from her mother while eyeballing a family with their faces buried in fudge sundaes. A reach into my homemade, Denim-shorts pocket reminded me that lint-balls nestled where money burned holes, leaving me penniless on a sweltering July afternoon with the entire tribe at Six Flags. Gawking at the feasting family, I felt that familiar twinge of jealousy I experienced as the kid of a welfare mom when visiting the plush homes she vacuumed and dusted in Dean Estates. I detested the possibility of my Olivia feeling that same envy I felt when watching the children of my mother's employer dive into their in-ground pools and climb their upscale tree houses. I didn't have faith to say what I was thinking: "I'll get you an ice cream before the close of this day." Instead, I made an effort to talk with her about something else that piqued her interest. Fun dialogue with your children adequately atones for whatever creature-comforts you can't give them. But still, I wanted her to have that freakin' ice cream.

Just before twilight, Olivia and I waited in line for over ten minutes only to discover that the ride was shutting down for repairs. A cloud of disappointment shoved the sun into obscurity, leaving us both feeling dreary. No ice-cream sundaes, no ride. Suddenly, a ray of light bolted over me when I noticed a uniformed Six Flags manager standing at the exit. At the sight of his badge, I heard the sound of opportunity knocking. Isn't it funny how the darkest moments set the stage for the brightest ideas? Face to face with the manager, I pled my case on how we traveled two hours for Olivia to enjoy her "favorite ride" (well, at least that's how I described it) only to realize it is inoperable. "Sir, the ride has malfunctioned. What would you like me to do?" he asked in a huffy tone. "Free ice-cream for the entire family," I replied unflinchingly. And oddly enough, he did just that.

After handing us several vouchers, we all buried our faces in decorative sundaes. With vanilla ice-cream drenched gummy bears pasted to her chin, Olivia offered me a grateful grin. When opportunity knocks, you don't always storm through an open door but sometimes crawl through a cracked basement window.

Key Bible Verse:

"Therefore be as shrewd as snakes and as innocent as doves" (Matt. 10:16).

SOCIAL MEDIA EXERCISE: Post on the *Pain Into Parables Facebook Group Page* a picture of your favorite parable from chapter four. Please share about how you relate to this parable from your own experiences. Also, please add, #PainIntoParables, at the conclusion of your post.

CHAPTER FIVE
Your Purpose—Others

So, why would Jesus order this lame man to pick up his mat and walk? In addition to all of the reasons we discussed, there remains another purpose that has nothing to do with the man's wellbeing.

When the man walked pass the invalids sprawled out on their own mats near the Pool of Bethsaida, he was probably instantly recognized by others. The mat he carried was a dead giveaway that he was once an invalid just like them.

According to their perspective, the mat signified who he was *before* Jesus showed up; an invalid stuck in one spot for thirty-eight years. His mobile feet signified who he was *after* Jesus showed up; a healed gentleman with new feet to try out.

By carrying his mat, the man offers a *Before and After Contrast* to the world around him of who he was before and after being touched by Love. Nothing exhibits a metamorphosis more vividly than seeing the before and after photos.

The final reason why Jesus commanded this man to carry his mat was for the sake of *Others*, so they could behold the transformation he endured.

Many moons ago, when General William Booth was unable to attend a conference hosted by the organization he founded, the Salvation Army, he delivered his message to the attendees at the conference by way of cable.

From his sick bed, he cabled one word: *Others!* Booth knew that the sole purpose of our lives, especially as believers in a higher power, was for the betterment of other people.

Think it not strange that Jesus would command for you to carry your mat. Consider it not bizarre that Jesus would ask for you to write down your story, own it and share it every chance you get. There are *Others* who frantically need to hear what you share.

It is arguable that an artist like German immigrant Carl Bersch painted a picture for his own pleasure; certainly, art has proven many therapeutic benefits.

It is debatable that a vocalist bellows out symphonies for her own satisfaction, as shower times have been shown to be far more relaxing when you sing tunes.

It is possible that gemcutters carve diamonds for their own enjoyment; kinesthetic activities release dopamine within the brain.

However, the artist, the vocalist and the gemcutter will probably tell you that the greatest pleasure is experienced when they watch others find pleasure in what they do. Likewise, the greatest pleasure for you will be to witness others benefit from your parables.

Like the work of art, the song, and the diamond, put your parables on display for *Others* to experience.

In the words of Jesus himself, "Neither do people light a lamp and put it under a bowl. Instead, they put it on its stand and it gives light to everyone in the house" (Matt. 5:15).

Practical Ways to Share Your Parables

—Write your parables down in a physical or digital journal. Make copies of that journal and assign copies to all your family and friends within a legal document (aka. Will) to be issued at the

time of your passing. Pass down your legacy of wisdom, acquired from hardships, to the people you love. Let your hindsight serve as their foresight.

—*Share your parables* on social media venues such as Facebook. More than likely, there are many others who suffer from the same plights you endured; people who need to know that they are not alone. One of the values of the recent *Me Too Movement* is that it let victims of sexual assault know that they had friends who went through similar ordeals. Sharing your parables lets people know that they can survive too, since you yourself survived.

—*Share your parables* in churches, prisons, schools, hospitals, nursing homes or whatever institution offers you the opportunity. Especially target those institutions that correlate to your narratives. For instance, if you were a lawbreaker at one time, seek for opportunities with the criminal population.

—*Write and publish* a book that features your pain translated into your own parables. Market that book to a demographic that relates to your story.

—*Create a podcast* of your parables and share that podcast on a website or other places online.

SOCIAL MEDIA EXERCISE: Post on the *Pain Into Parables Facebook Group Page* your own finished parable along with any image that captures the essence of your parable. Please add, #PainIntoParables, at the conclusion of your post.

One Final Parable

"You're the guy who stole a police cruiser, landing yourself in juvenile jail!" Steve hollers across the church foyer in his thick, Italo-American brogue while I try to hide behind the nearest coat-rack. "You're the guy once on all those prescription drugs!" he shouts like I'm seven football fields away in a vestibule no larger than the conventional living-room.

I'm no stranger to deafening voices; most of my Guido-relatives sound like they swallowed a microphone too. But I'm trying my best to preserve my anonymity within this new church.

"Shhh! Can you please keep your voice down when discussing these matters?" I ask while scanning my surroundings for any news-bags. The reason why I feel so comfortable here is because nobody knows me from the corners on which I lingered or the streets down which I roamed. Isn't it true that oftentimes, we embark upon new places in order to hit the reset button on the old places?

One of the primary reasons I joined this church family was to run away from the past eighteen years. After multiple hospitalizations for suicide attempts along with incarceration for grand theft auto, I yearned for a fresh start in life. But my attempt to dash from my past was much like some terrified female running from Michael Meyers in one of those Halloween flicks.

As the victim runs for her life, gasping for air, she foolishly presumes she's gained headway from the monster *behind* her when he suddenly pops up *before* her. "Where the heck did he come from! I thought I got away from him?" she shockingly thinks.

That's what it looks like when you run from your past.

You assume you've gained mileage from the ghosts behind you when they startlingly pop up before you!

"But I don't understand, Mike? Why don't you want to talk about these things?" he asks in a volume slightly quieter than his hollering. Haven't you read Nathaniel Hawthorne's *The Scarlet Letter*? I wanted to ask, but didn't think he would comprehend the reference. "Maybe a little shame." I reply.

Staring into my eyes unflinchingly, he says "Any story that highlights the pits from whence Jesus dug you is a story that you don't whisper in a corner, but you shout from a rooftop!"

Enough said. Who would have imagined, in that moment back in the Fall of 1996, that I would invest the next twenty-three years in the roofing business?

"You are the light of the world.
A town built on a hill cannot be hidden.
Neither do people light a lamp and put it under a bowl.
Instead, they put it on its stand,
and it gives light to everyone in the house.
In the same way, let your light shine before others,
that they may see your good deeds and
glorify your Father in heaven."

(Matt. 5:14-16)

Acknowledgments

To my Father in heaven, it was Your mighty hand that plucked me out of the many pits along the way (even those pits I leaped into), it was Your grace that sustained me, and it was Your plan to predestine me for greatness.

To my parents, Michael and Dawn, despite your youthfulness, it was your continual efforts of love and commitment that instilled confidence within me.

To my children, Ashley, Mikie, Hannah and Olivia, it was your arrival on this planet that motivated me to be a better man.

To my Aunt Rose, it was your hospitality that kept me sane during one of the most trying times of my life, and throughout the writing of this book.

To my grandfather, Fred, it was the memory of sitting on your lap, striking the keys on your typewriter, that inspired me to be an author. You left me your mantle when you went home.

To Colleen Mellor, it was your tenacious investment in my tenth grade English class that caused me to win a state-wide award and take my writing skills seriously.

To Bishop Jeff Williams, it was your words: "Stop treating it like a hobby! Start treating it like an assignment!" that helped me get the job done.

To my older brother, Scott Axtmann, it was your discipleship that taught me how to pray, fast, read my Bible and love people unconditionally.

To my spiritual father, Pasco Manzo, it was your leadership, mentorship, and role-modeling that made a man out of me on every level of my life.

To my opponents, with all forgiveness, sincerity, and love, I owe you a letter of gratitude for the opportunities you gave me to grow in Christ-likeness.

 *With additional thanks to*

Andrew Rock of *Envelope Stories* for editorial advice.

William Armitage of *Words in the Works* for book design.

Rebecca Danielle of *Radiance by Rebecca Photography* for the photographs of Michael.

Simone Spruce of *simonespruce.com* for the title page illustration.

About the Author

Michael A. Caparrelli, PhD (abd) served for sixteen years as a pastor of a recovery church in Rhode Island. Currently, he is in the final dissertation stage of his PhD in Behavioral Science, investigating the impact of church on the recovery journey of adults with addictions.

He travels across the nation, speaking to churches, schools, prisons and rehabs, on a variety of subjects in behavioral health from a faith-based perspective.

He has four children–Ashley, Mikie, Hannah and Olivia. He is a devout follower of Jesus Christ.

If you would like to book Michael for a speaking engagement, please email him at: Michaelcaparrelli@unmuted.app

P.I.C.T.U.R.E *Workbook*

A specially-formatted workbook is available online to accompany this book: *Pen Your Pain Into Parables—A Tool for Recovery Workbook*

P – *Pain*

_____

_____

_____

_____

_____

_____

_____

_____

_____

_____

_____

_____

_____

_____

_____

_____

_____

_____

_____

_____

_____

_____

I – Incident

C – Conflict

_____

_____

_____

_____

_____

_____

_____

_____

_____

_____

_____

_____

_____

_____

_____

_____

_____

_____

_____

_____

_____

_____

_____

_____

T – Truth

U – *Unfolding Action*

R – Resolution

E – Empathy

A specially-formatted workbook is available online to accompany this book: *Pen Your Pain Into Parables–A Tool for Recovery Workbook*

Made in the USA
Middletown, DE
20 April 2022

64531743R00083